Liberia	Libya	Liechtenstein	Lithuania	Luxembourg	Macedonia, FYRO	Madagascar
Malawi	Malaysia	Maldives	Mali	Malta	Marshall Islands	Mauritania
Mauritius	Mexico	Micronesia	Moldova	Monaco	Mongolia	Montenegro
Morocco	Mozambique	Myanmar	Namibia	Nauru	Nepal	Netherlands
New Zealand	Nicaragua	Niger	Nigeria	Northern Marianas	North Korea	Norway
Oman	Pakistan	Palau	Panama	Papua New Guinea	Paraguay	Peru
Philippines	Poland	Portugal	Qatar	Romania	Russian Federation	Rwanda
St. Kitts and Nevis	St. Lucia	St. Vincent & the Grenadines	Samoa	San Marino	Sao Tomé and Principe	Saudi Arabia
Senegal	Serbia	Seychelles	Sierra Leone	Singapore	Slovakia	Slovenia
Solomon Islands	Somalia	South Africa	South Korea	Spain	Sri Lanka	Sudan
Suriname	Swaziland	Sweden	Switzerland	Syria	Taiwan	Tajikistan
Tanzania	Thailand	Togo	Tonga	Trinidad and Tobago	Tunisia	Turkey
Turkmenistan	Uganda	Ukraine	United Arab Emirates	United Kingdom	United States of America	Uruguay
Uzbekistan	Vanuatu	Venezuela	Vietnam	Yemen	Zambia	Zimbabwe

Oxford Primary Atlas

Editorial Adviser

Dr Patrick Wiegand

OXFORD
UNIVERSITY PRESS

Great Clarendon Street, Oxford OX2 6DP

Oxford University Press is a department of the University of Oxford.
It furthers the University's objective of excellence in research, scholarship,
and education by publishing worldwide in

Oxford   New York

Auckland Cape Town Dar es Salaam Hong Kong Karachi
Kuala Lumpur Madrid Melbourne Mexico City Nairobi
New Delhi Shanghai Taipei Toronto

With offices in

Argentina Austria Brazil Chile Czech Republic France Greece
Guatemala Hungary Italy Japan Poland Portugal Singapore
South Korea Switzerland Thailand Turkey Ukraine Vietnam

Oxford is a registered trade mark of Oxford University Press
in the UK and in certain other countries

ISBN 978 0 19 848016 7 (hardback)

ISBN 978 0 19 848017 4 (paperback)

1 3 5 7 9 10 8 6 4 2

Printed in Singapore by KHL Printing Co. Pte Ltd.

TEACHERS
For inspirational support plus
free resources and eBooks
www.oxfordprimary.co.uk

PARENTS
Help your child's reading
with essential tips, fun
activities and free eBooks
www.oxfordowl.co.uk

Acknowledgments

The publisher and author would like to thank the following:

p5br: ICP/Alamy; **p8t:** Robert Harding Picture Library Ltd/Alamy; **p8tc:** The Photolibrary Wales/Alamy; **p8c:** Geogphotos/Alamy; **p8bc:** Ivan J Belcher/Worldwide Picture Library/Alamy; **p8b:** Chinch Gryniewicz/Corbis; **p9tr:** Jonathan Dorey - Scotland/Alamy; **p9cl:** Andy Stothert/Britain on View/Photolibrary.com; **p9bl:** Graham Oliver/Alamy; **p9br:** Realimage/Alamy; **p10tl:** Jason Hawkes Aerial Photography; **p10tr:** Sefton Samuels/Rex Features; **p10cr:** David Goddard/Getty Images; **p10bl:** Derek Rees/Photolibrary Wales; **p10br:** Steve Benbow Photolibrary Wales; **p11tl:** Planetary Visions Ltd/Science Photo Library; **p11tr:** Roger Ressmeyer/Corbis; **p11bl:** NASA/age Fotostock/Photolibrary.com; **p11br:** NASA; **p12:** PlanetObserver/Science Photo Library; **p16:** PlanetObserver/Science Photo Library; **p17:** James McNie; **p18t:** Tomasz Szatewicz/ Alamy; **p18b:** Michael David Murphy/Alamy; **p19:** North News; **p20:** Russell Kord/Alamy; **p21br:** Simon Margetson/Alamy; **p21bl:** Ingolf Pompe 5/Alamy; **p21br:** Pakimon/Shutterstock; **p23:** Pawel Osinski/iStockphoto.com; **p24:** Superstock Inc/ Photolibrary.com; **p26:** Liquid Light/Alamy; **p29:** John Boud/Alamy; **p30:** Philip Fenton/Britain on View /Photolibrary.com; **p32t:** David Crausby/Alamy; **p32c:** Elmtree Images/Alamy; **p32b:** Patrick Ingrand/Stone/Getty Images; **p33t:** Clynt Garnham Renewable Energy/ Alamy; **p33c:** Pixtal Images/Photolibrary.com; **p33b:** Neil lee Sharp/Alamy; **p34t:** Brenton West/Alamy; **p34b:** Digital Vision/Getty Images; **p35tr:** Tony Page/Stone/Getty Images; **p35cr:** Jon Arnold Images Ltd/Alamy; **p35bl:** Chris Demetriou/Frank Lane Picture Agency; **p35cl:** Ian Thraves/Alamy; **p36l:** David Martyn Hughes/Alamy; **p36c:** Jason Hawkes Aerial Photography; **p36r:** G P Bowater/Alamy; **p37t:** Martin Jones/Corbis; **p37tc:** The Trustees Of The British Museum/British Museum Images; **p37bc:** Herbert Kehrer/imagebroker.net/ Photolibrary.com; **p37b:** Richard

Cooke/Taxi/Getty Images; **p40:** Phil Dunne/Alamy; **p42:** Carmen Sedano/Alamy; **p46:** Jagadeesh/Reuters/Corbis; **p49:** Emma Sklar/Rex Features; **p52:** Yann Arthus-Bertrand/ Corbis; **p53:** Daryl Balfour/ABPL/Animals Animals/ Photolibrary.com; **p57:** James Randklev/ Photographer's Choice/Getty Images; **p60:** Pascal Rondeau/Stone/Getty Images; **p64l:** Image Makers/The Image Bank/Getty Images; **p64r:** NPA/Stone/Getty Images; **p65l:** Earth Satellite Corporation/Science Photo Library; **p65r:** Planetary Visions Ltd/Science Photo Library; **p68cl:** Mediacolor's/Alamy; **p68tl:** Radius Images/Photolibrary.com; **p68tr:** Ron Watts/Corbis; **p68bl:** Ashfordplatt/Alamy; **p68br:** Charles & Josette Lenars/Corbis; **p69tl:** John Warburton-Lee Photography/Photolibrary.com; **p69tr:** Richard A. Cooke/Documentary Value/Corbis; **p69bl:** Wolfgang Kaehler/Corbis; **p69bc:** Galen Rowell/Terra/Corbis; **p69br:** Frans Lemmens/The Image Bank/Getty Images; **p70bl:** Jan Krimmer/imagebroker.net/ Photolibrary.com; **p70br:** Christian Heinrich/imagebroker RF/Photolibrary.com; **p71bl:** Ben Osborne/Stone/Getty Images; **p71br:** Fawzan Husain/Photolibrary.com; **p71cr:** Neale Clarke/Robert Harding Travel/ Photolibrary.com

Images sourced by Pictureresearch.co.uk

Illustrations by Mark Brierley p66 (icons); Mark Duffin p5 (compass), p59; Gary Hincks p8, p9; Harry Venning p66

Cover photo by Magskyphoto/Shutterstock. Cover globe by Jan Rysavy/iStockphoto

2 Contents

- Understanding the Earth ———— 4
- Understanding direction ———— 5
- Understanding maps ———— 6–7
- Understanding land height ———— 8
- Understanding rivers ———— 9
- Understanding settlements ———— 10
- Understanding satellite images — 11

World

Satellite image ———— 12–13
Countries and continents ———— 14–15

The British Isles

Satellite image ———— 16
Geography ———— 17
Land and rivers ———— 18
Weather and climate ———— 19
Countries ———— 20

The United Kingdom

United Kingdom and
the European Union ———— 21

Northern Scotland ———— 22–23

Northern Ireland and
Southern Scotland ———— 24

Southern Scotland and
Northern England ———— 25

Wales ———— 26

Midlands ———— 27

South East England ———— 28–29

South West England ———— 30–31

People and cities ———— 32

Energy ———— 33

Pollution and recycling ———— 34

Conservation ———— 35

Connections ———— 36

Holidays and tourism ———— 37

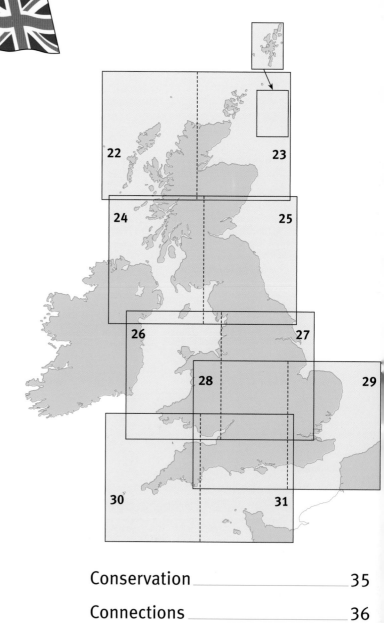

Contents

Europe

Land and rivers	38
Countries	39
Northern Europe	40–41
Southern Europe	42–43

Asia

Land and rivers	44
Countries	45
India, Pakistan and Bangladesh	46–47
China and Japan	48–49

Africa

Land and rivers	50
Countries	51
Egypt	52
East Africa	53

North America

Land and rivers	54
Countries	55
United States of America	56–57

South America

Land and rivers	58
Countries	59
Brazil, Peru, Bolivia	60–61

Oceania

Land and rivers	62
Countries	62

The Poles

The Arctic Ocean	63
Antarctica	63

World

Satellite image	12–13
Countries and continents	14–15
Land and rivers	64–65
Climate	66–67
Environments	68–69
Environmental problems	70–71
People and cities	72–73
Connections	74–75
• Country data files	76–77
• Index	78–80

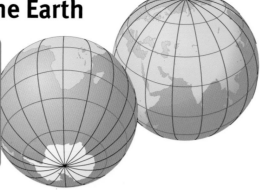

The Earth is a planet in space. It is a sphere. Two sets of imaginary lines help us describe where places are on the surface of the Earth.

Latitude

Lines of latitude measure distance north or south of the equator.

The **Equator** is at latitude 0°.

The **Poles** are at latitude 90°N and 90°S.

Can you find the **Equator**, the **Prime Meridian** and the **International Date Line** on a globe?

North Pole
Arctic Circle
60°N
40°N
Tropic of Cancer
20°N
0° Equator
20°S
Tropic of Capricorn
40°S
60°S
Antarctic Circle
South Pole

Longitude

Lines of longitude measure distance eas or west of the Prime Meridian.

The **Prime Meridian** (also called the Greenwich Meridian) is at longitude 0°.

The **International Date Line** (on the other side of the Earth) is based on longitude 180°.

60°W 40°W 20°W 0° 20°E 40°E
Prime Meridian

There are many ways of showing the spherical Earth on a flat world map.

Map projections

How a world map looks depends on where it is going to be used.

World map used in the United Kingdom and Europe

World map used in Australia and New Zealand

Can you find Antarctica on a globe and compare how it looks on a world map?

Grid codes

In this atlas, the lines of latitude and longitude are used to make a grid.

The columns of the grid have letters.

The rows of the grid have numbers.

Numbers and letters together make a **grid code** that can be used to describe where places are on the Earth.

Can you name the city at gridcode **B2**?

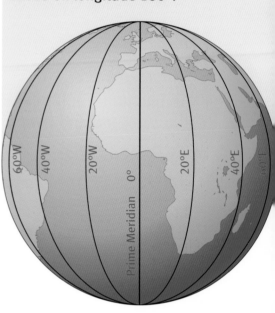

Casablanca
MOROCCO
Tripoli
Cairo
EGYPT
Tropic of Cancer
ALGERIA
LIBYA
MALI
NIGER
CHAD
Khartoum
SUDAN
Monrovia
Abuja
ETHIOPIA
Mogadishu
Equator
KENYA
DEMOCRATIC REPUBLIC OF CONGO
TANZANIA
Dodoma
ATLANTIC OCEAN
Luanda
INDIAN OCEAN
ANGOLA
ZAMBIA
MADAGASCAR
Tropic of Capricorn
NAMIBIA
BOTSWANA
REPUBLIC OF SOUTH AFRICA
Durban
Cape Town
SOUTHERN OCEAN
Prime Meridian
MEDITERRANEAN SEA

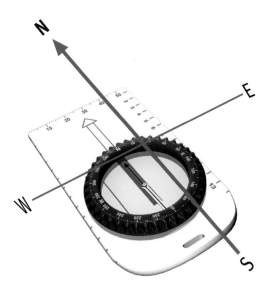

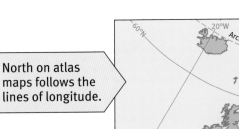

A compass is used for finding direction. The needle of a compass always points north.

Which way is North?

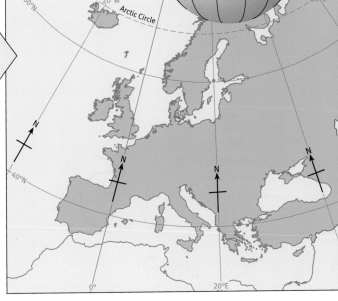

North on atlas maps follows the lines of longitude.

London is north of Brighton.

Brighton is south of London.

Reading is west of London.

Portsmouth is south west of London.

Using a compass, can you find which direction north is from where you are?

Global Positioning System (GPS) satellites send signals to equipment on the ground. When a GPS receiver, such as SatNav in a car, picks up signals from several satellites it can work out where it is and give directions to where you want to go.

How does SatNav work?

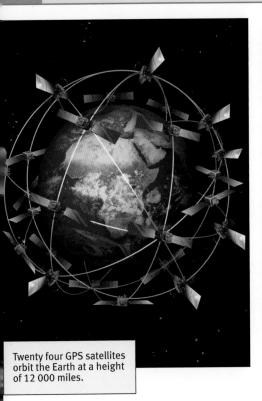

Twenty four GPS satellites orbit the Earth at a height of 12 000 miles.

A SatNav receiver has to be able to 'see' at least four satellites to work out where it is.

Tell SatNav where you want to go and it gives you directions. This one has a moving map as well as voice instructions.

6 Understanding maps

⊙ Special words are used to describe parts of maps.

Map language

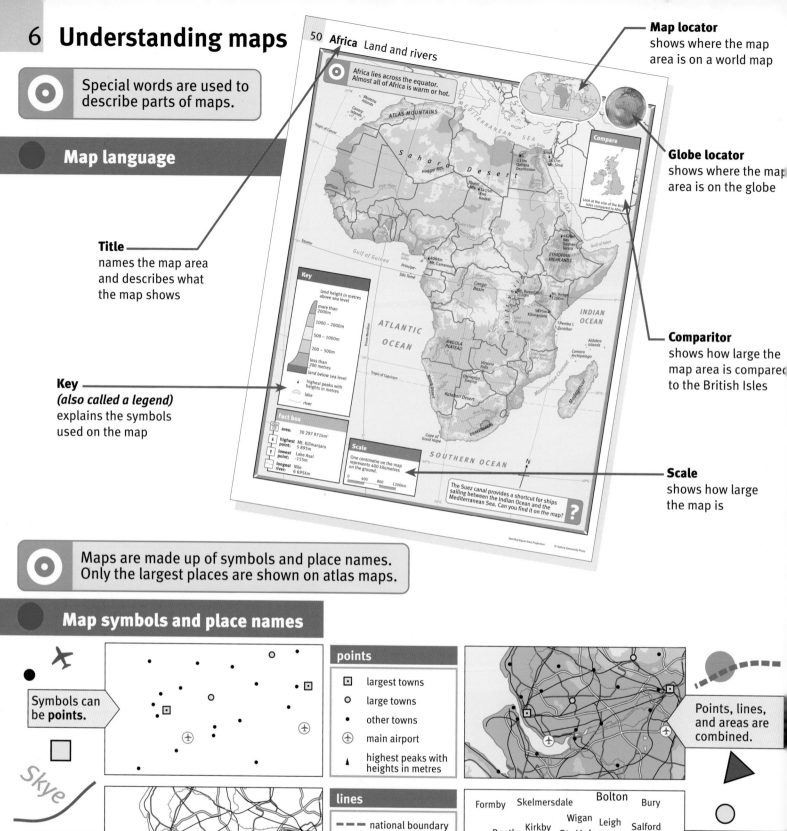

Title
names the map area and describes what the map shows

Key
(also called a legend)
explains the symbols used on the map

Map locator
shows where the map area is on a world map

Globe locator
shows where the map area is on the globe

Comparitor
shows how large the map area is compared to the British Isles

Scale
shows how large the map is

⊙ Maps are made up of symbols and place names. Only the largest places are shown on atlas maps.

Map symbols and place names

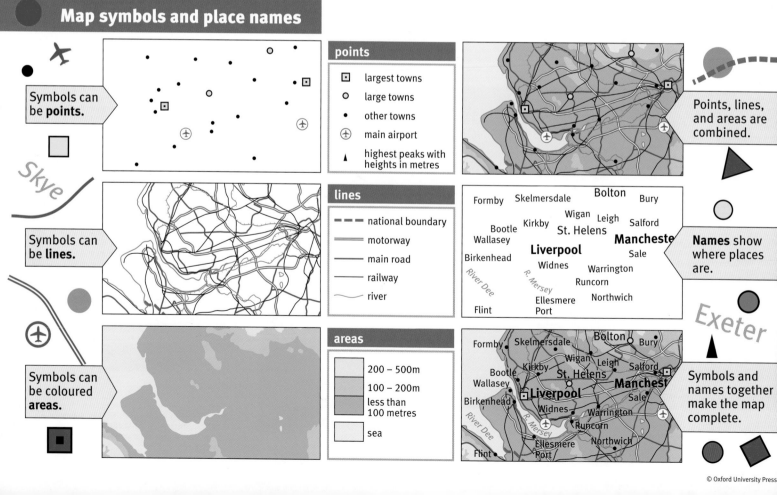

Symbols can be **points**.

Symbols can be **lines**.

Symbols can be coloured **areas**.

points

⊡	largest towns
○	large towns
•	other towns
⊕	main airport
▲	highest peaks with heights in metres

lines

▬ ▬	national boundary
═	motorway
─	main road
─	railway
～	river

areas

	200 – 500m
	100 – 200m
	less than 100 metres
	sea

Points, lines, and areas are combined.

Names show where places are.

Symbols and names together make the map complete.

© Oxford University Press

The way names are printed on maps gives an important clue to what sorts of places they describe.

Type on maps

Great Britain *Ireland*	islands
UNITED KINGDOM **REPUBLIC OF IRELAND**	countries
ENGLAND **SCOTLAND** **WALES** **NORTHERN IRELAND**	parts of the United Kingdom
PENNINES *GRAMPIAN MOUNTAINS*	physical features
Ben Nevis Snowdon	mountain peaks
NORTH SEA *English Channel*	sea areas
Manchester York Dover	settlements

An abbreviation is a shortened version of a word or a group of words.

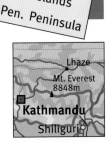

R.	River
Mt.	Mount
Is.	Islands
Pen.	Peninsula

Map abbreviations

Some country names are abbreviated using the first letters of each word

UK	United Kingdom
USA	United States of America
UAE	United Arab Emirates

Atlas maps are much, much smaller than the places they show. A few centimetres on the map stand for very many kilometres on the ground.

Scale

Each division on the scale line is one centimetre. The scale line shows how many kilometres are represented by one centimetre.

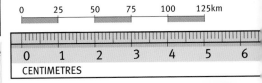

| 0 | 25 | 50 | 75 | 100 | 125km |

| 0 | 1 | 2 | 3 | 4 | 5 | 6 |

CENTIMETRES

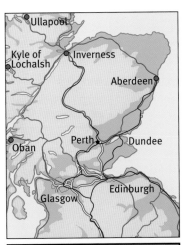

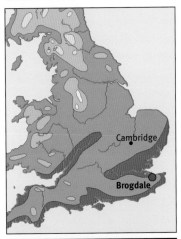

Scale
One centimetre on the map represents **25** kilometres on the ground.

0   25   50   75km

The distance between Bangor and Betws-y-Coed is about 25km

Scale
One centimetre on the map represents **50** kilometres on the ground.

0   50   100   150km

The distance between Perth and Edinburgh is about 50km

Scale
One centimetre on the map represents **100** kilometres on the ground.

0   100   200   300km

The distance between Cambridge and Brogdale is about 100km

Larger scale
smaller area
more detail

Smaller scale
larger area
less detail

Choose a map from this atlas. Can you use a ruler to work out the distance in kilometres between two places?   **?**

On atlas maps the height of the land is shown by colours.

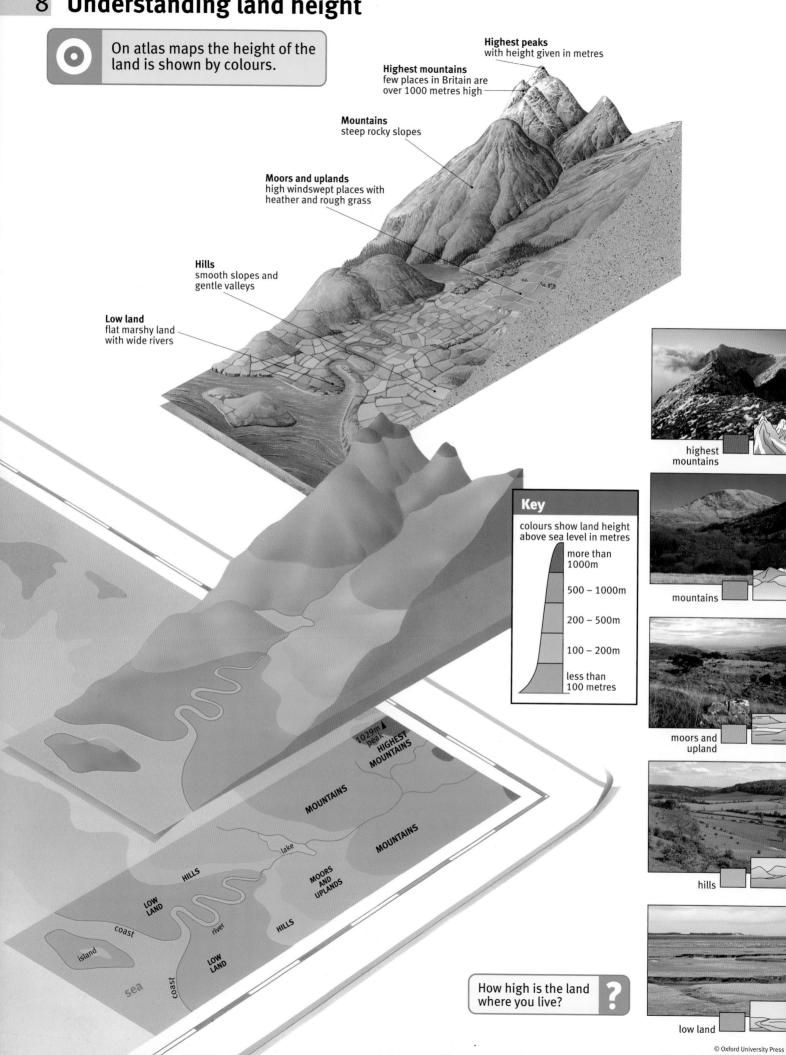

Highest peaks
with height given in metres

Highest mountains
few places in Britain are over 1000 metres high

Mountains
steep rocky slopes

Moors and uplands
high windswept places with heather and rough grass

Hills
smooth slopes and gentle valleys

Low land
flat marshy land with wide rivers

Key

colours show land height above sea level in metres

more than 1000m

500 – 1000m

200 – 500m

100 – 200m

less than 100 metres

1029m peak
HIGHEST MOUNTAINS

MOUNTAINS

MOUNTAINS

lake

MOORS AND UPLANDS

HILLS

HILLS

LOW LAND

HILLS

LOW LAND

coast

river

coast

island

sea

highest mountains

mountains

moors and upland

hills

low land

How high is the land where you live?

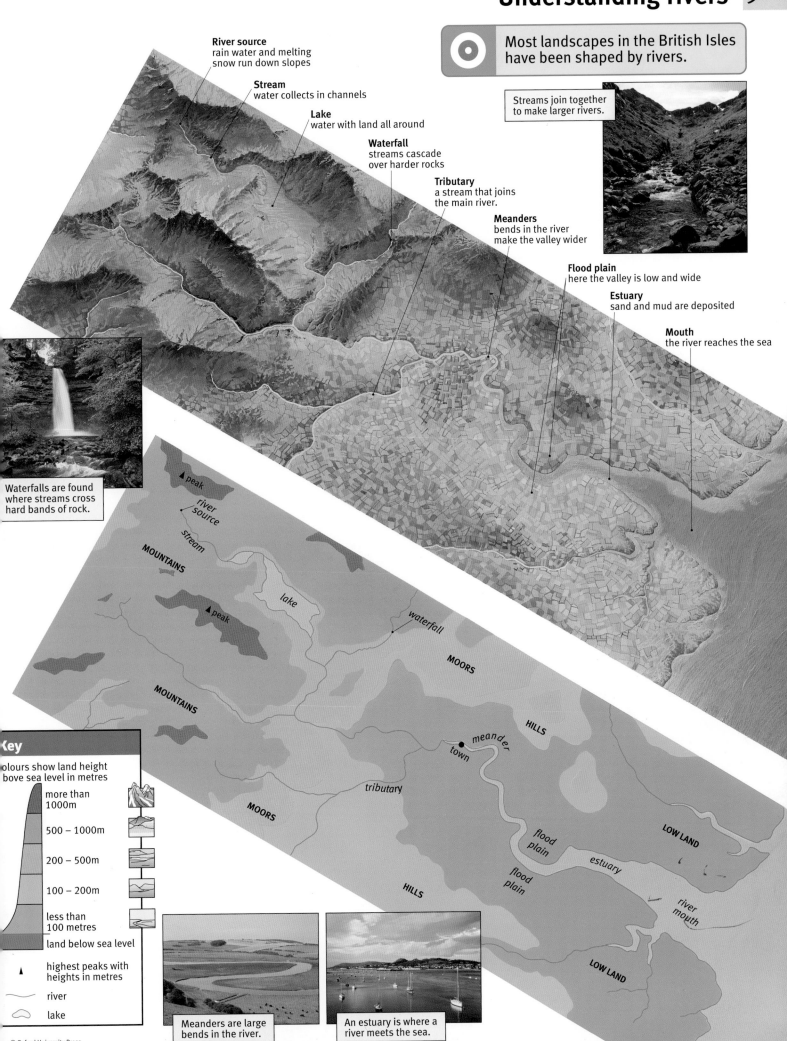

Most landscapes in the British Isles have been shaped by rivers.

Streams join together to make larger rivers.

River source
rain water and melting snow run down slopes

Stream
water collects in channels

Lake
water with land all around

Waterfall
streams cascade over harder rocks

Tributary
a stream that joins the main river.

Meanders
bends in the river make the valley wider

Flood plain
here the valley is low and wide

Estuary
sand and mud are deposited

Mouth
the river reaches the sea

Waterfalls are found where streams cross hard bands of rock.

peak

river source

stream

MOUNTAINS

peak

lake

waterfall

MOORS

HILLS

MOUNTAINS

town

meander

MOORS

tributary

flood plain

flood plain

estuary

LOW LAND

HILLS

river mouth

LOW LAND

Key

Colours show land height above sea level in metres

more than 1000m

500 – 1000m

200 – 500m

100 – 200m

less than 100 metres

land below sea level

▲ highest peaks with heights in metres

river

lake

Meanders are large bends in the river.

An estuary is where a river meets the sea.

© Oxford University Press

🎯 People live in settlements of different sizes.
Most people in Britain live in towns and cities.

Largest towns
⊡ Very tall office buildings mark the
centre of the largest towns.

Largest built-up areas
Several towns and cities have grown
together to make one continuous
built up area.

Large towns
○ Larger settlements have more shops
and services than smaller ones.

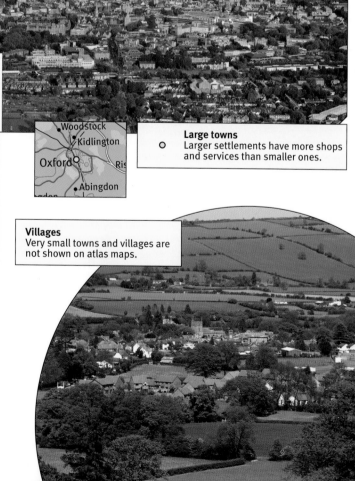

Villages
Very small towns and villages are
not shown on atlas maps.

Other towns
• In smaller towns the countryside is
never far away from the centre.

What size of settlement do
you live in? **?**

> Satellite images are pictures of the Earth taken from space. They help us understand the weather, our environment and the Earth itself.

Hundreds of working satellites orbit the Earth. There are also thousands that don't work any more, called 'space junk'.

During the year many wet weather fronts pass over the British Isles whilst France and Spain stay warm and dry. Compare this satellite image with the maps on pages 38 and 39.

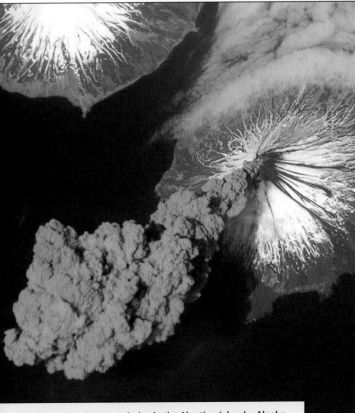

A snow-covered volcano explodes in the Aleutian Islands, Alaska. The cloud of ash was three miles high. Can you find the Aleutian islands on the world map on page 64?

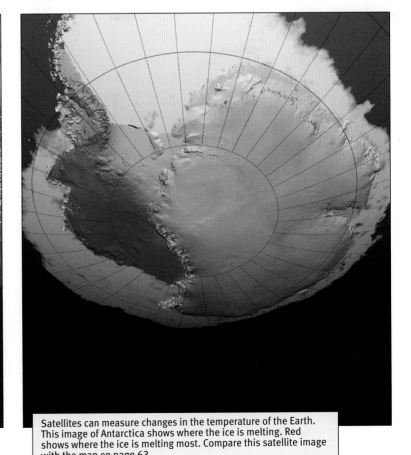

Satellites can measure changes in the temperature of the Earth. This image of Antarctica shows where the ice is melting. Red shows where the ice is melting most. Compare this satellite image with the map on page 63.

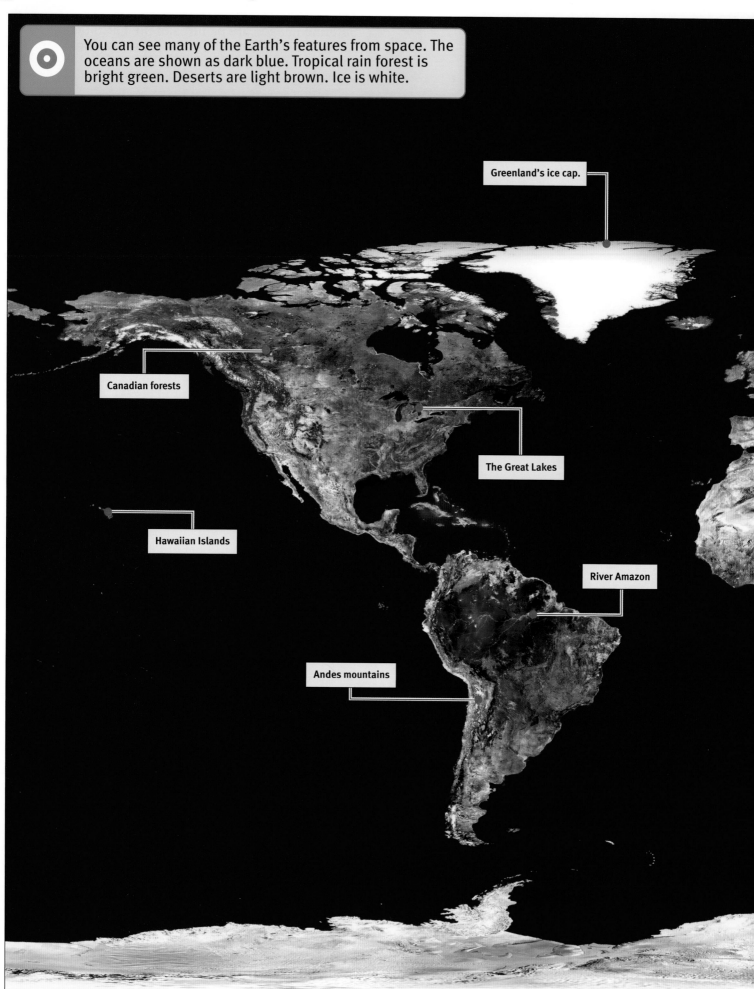

You can see many of the Earth's features from space. The oceans are shown as dark blue. Tropical rain forest is bright green. Deserts are light brown. Ice is white.

Greenland's ice cap.

Canadian forests

The Great Lakes

Hawaiian Islands

River Amazon

Andes mountains

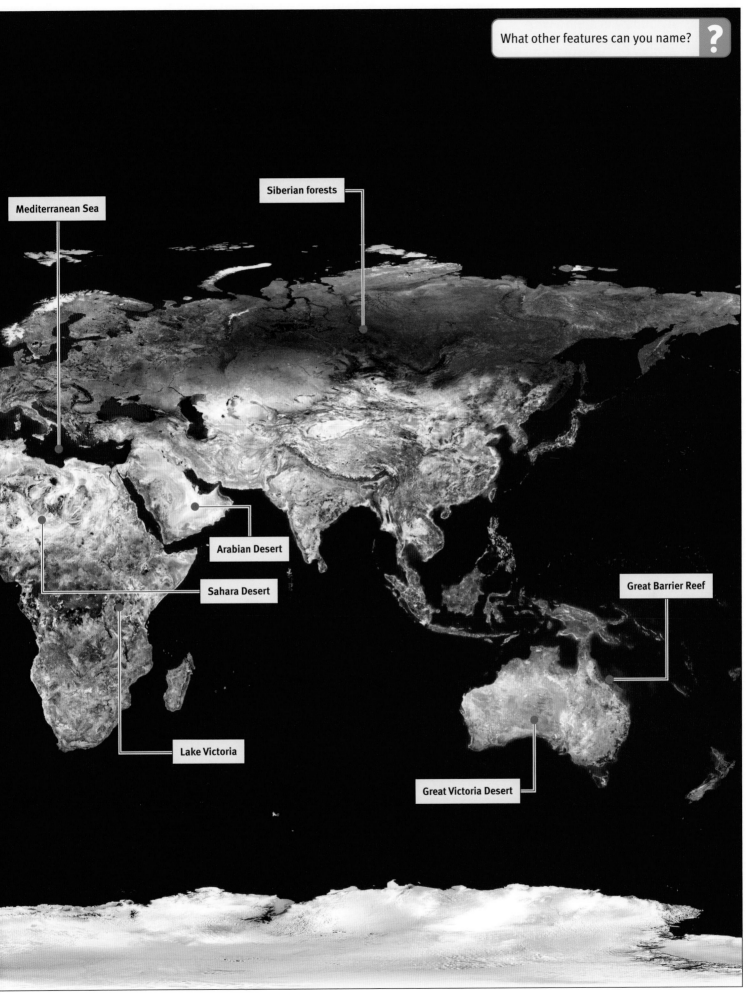

What other features can you name? **?**

Siberian forests

Mediterranean Sea

Arabian Desert

Sahara Desert

Great Barrier Reef

Lake Victoria

Great Victoria Desert

A country is a land with its own people and its own laws. A capital city is the most important city in a country. It is where the government meets.

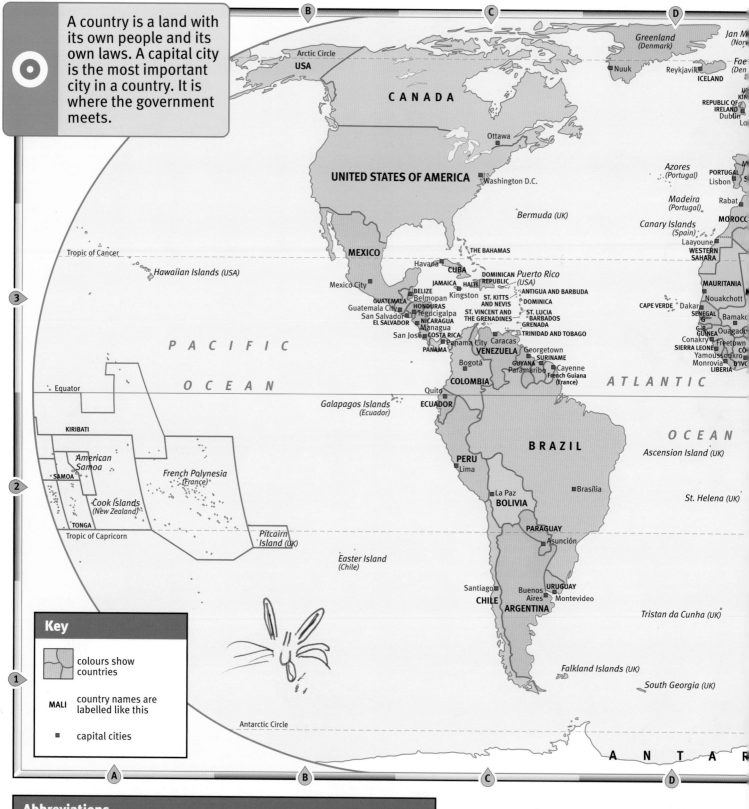

B
C
D

Arctic Circle

USA

Greenland
(Denmark)

Jan M
(Nor

Nuuk

Reykjavik
ICELAND

Fae
(Den

C A N A D A

REPUBLIC OF
IRELAND
Dublin
Lo

Ottawa

UNITED STATES OF AMERICA Washington D.C.

Bermuda (UK)

*Azores
(Portugal)*

PORTUGAL
Lisbon

*Madeira
(Portugal)*

Rabat

KIN

Tropic of Cancer

Hawaiian Islands (USA)

MEXICO

Havana
CUBA
THE BAHAMAS

*Canary Islands
(Spain)*

Laayoune
**WESTERN
SAHARA**

MOROCC

Mexico City

JAMAICA
HAITI

**DOMINICAN
REPUBLIC**

*Puerto Rico
(USA)*

MAURITANIA

Nouakchott

3

Kingston

ANTIGUA AND BARBUDA
DOMINICA

Dakar

BELIZE
Belmopan
GUATEMALA
Guatemala City
San Salvador
EL SALVADOR

HONDURAS
Tegucigalpa
NICARAGUA
Managua

**ST. KITTS
AND NEVIS**

CAPE VERDE

SENEGAL

ST. LUCIA
ST. VINCENT AND
BARBADOS
THE GRENADINES
GRENADA

Conakry
SIERRA LEONE

G-B
GUINEA

Ouagadougou

CO

Freetown
Yamoussoukro

COSTA RICA
San José

TRINIDAD AND TOBAGO

D'IVO

PANAMA
Panama City
Caracas
VENEZUELA

Georgetown
SURINAME

Monrovia
LIBERIA

P A C I F I C

Bogotá

GUYANA
Paramaribo

Cayenne
*French Guiana
(France)*

A T L A N T I C

COLOMBIA
Quito

Equator

O C E A N

ECUADOR

*Galapagos Islands
(Ecuador)*

O C E A N

Ascension Island (UK)

KIRIBATI

B R A Z I L

PERU
Lima

*American
Samoa*

*French Polynesia
(France)*

La Paz

Brasília

St. Helena (UK)

2

SAMOA

BOLIVIA

*Cook Islands
(New Zealand)*

TONGA

Tropic of Capricorn

*Pitcairn
Island (UK)*

PARAGUAY

Asunción

*Easter Island
(Chile)*

Santiago
CHILE

Buenos
Aires
ARGENTINA

URUGUAY
Montevideo

Tristan da Cunha (UK)

Falkland Islands (UK)

South Georgia (UK)

Antarctic Circle

A
B
C
D

N
A
A R

Abbreviations

A	ALBANIA	G	THE GAMBIA	Q	QATAR	
AR	ARMENIA	G-B	GUINEA-BISSAU	R	ROMANIA	
AU	AUSTRIA	H	HUNGARY	S	SLOVAKIA	
AZ	AZERBAIJAN	IS	ISRAEL	SE	SERBIA	
B	BELGIUM	K	KOSOVO	SL	SLOVENIA	
BE	BENIN	L	LEBANON	SW	SWITZERLAND	
BH	BOSNIA-HERZEGOVINA	LI	LITHUANIA	T	TAJIKISTAN	
BR	BRUNEI	LU	LUXEMBOURG	TU	TURKMENISTAN	
BU	BURKINA	M	FORMER YUGOSLAV	U	UGANDA	
C	CROATIA		REPUBLIC OF MACEDONIA	UAE	UNITED ARAB EMIRATES	
CAR	CENTRAL AFRICAN REPUBLIC	MT	MONTENEGRO	ZIM	ZIMBABWE	
CZ	CZECH REPUBLIC	N	NETHERLANDS			

North America

South America

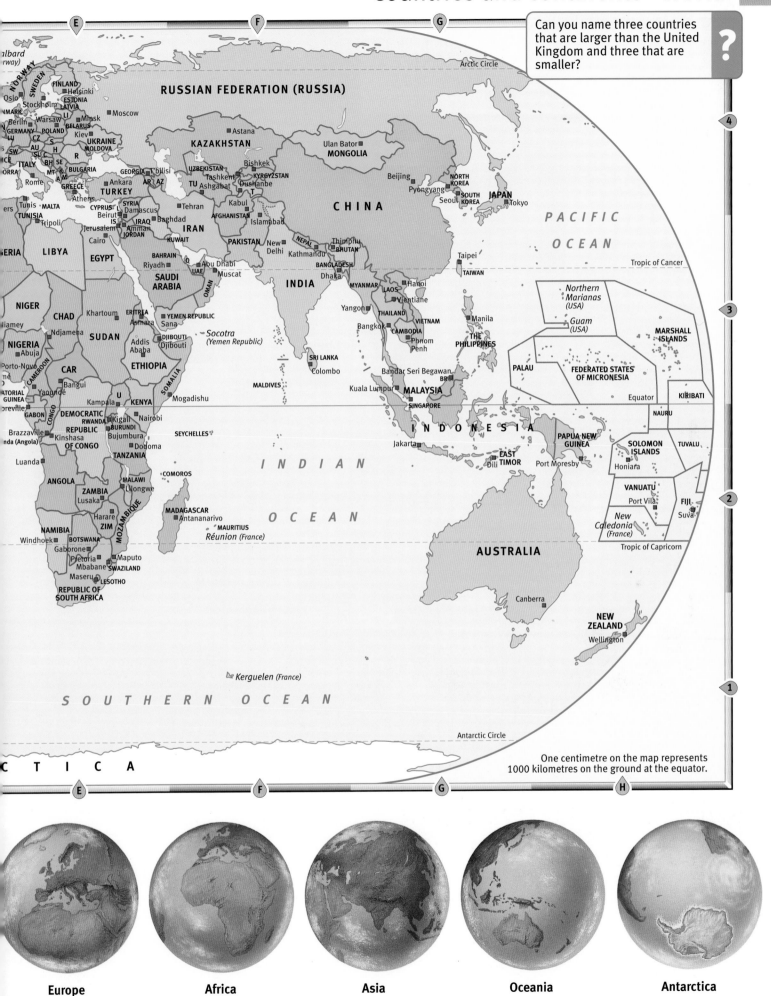

Can you name three countries that are larger than the United Kingdom and three that are smaller?

?

RUSSIAN FEDERATION (RUSSIA)

NORWAY
SWEDEN
FINLAND
Oslo
Helsinki
Stockholm
ESTONIA
LATVIA
DENMARK
Moscow
Berlin
Warsaw
Minsk
LI
GERMANY
POLAND
BELARUS
LU
Kiev
CZ
UKRAINE
S
AU
MOLDOVA
Astana
SL
H
R
ITALY
BH
SE
A M
BULGARIA
Rome
MT
GEORGIA
T'bilisi
GREECE
ANKARA
AR
AZ
TURKEY
Athens
SYRIA
CYPRUS
Beirut
Damascus
TU
MALTA
Tunis
IS
Baghdad
TUNISIA
Tripoli
Jerusalem
IRAQ
IRAN
Cairo
JORDAN
Amman
KUWAIT
LIBYA
EGYPT
BAHRAIN
Riyadh
Abu Dhabi
UAE
Muscat
SAUDI
ARABIA
OMAN

KAZAKHSTAN
Bishkek
UZBEKISTAN
Tashkent
KYRGYZSTAN
Ashgabat
Dushanbe
T
AFGHANISTAN
Kabul
Islamabad
PAKISTAN
New
Delhi
NEPAL
Kathmandu

Ulan Bator
MONGOLIA

Beijing
Pyongyang
NORTH
KOREA
SOUTH
KOREA
Seoul
JAPAN
Tokyo

CHINA

Thimphu
BHUTAN
BANGLADESH
Dhaka
INDIA
MYANMAR
Hanoi
LAOS
Yangon
Vientiane
THAILAND
VIETNAM
Bangkok
Manila
CAMBODIA
THE
PHILIPPINES
Phnom
Penh

Taipei
TAIWAN

PACIFIC

OCEAN

Tropic of Cancer

Northern
Marianas
(USA)
Guam
(USA)
MARSHALL
ISLANDS
PALAU
FEDERATED STATES
OF MICRONESIA
KIRIBATI
Equator
NAURU

NIGER
CHAD
Niamey
Ndjamena
SUDAN
Khartoum
ERITREA
Asmara
YEMEN REPUBLIC
Sana
Socotra
(Yemen Republic)
NIGERIA
Abuja
Porto-Novo
CAR
Bangui
CAMEROON
Yaoundé
ETHIOPIA
Addis
Ababa
DJIBOUTI
Djibouti
SRI LANKA
Colombo
MALDIVES
SOMALIA
EQUATORIAL
GUINEA
U
KENYA
Kampala
Mogadishu
GABON
Libreville
DEMOCRATIC
REPUBLIC
Kigali
RWANDA
Nairobi
Brazzaville
BURUNDI
Kinshasa
Bujumbura
CONGO
OF CONGO
Dodoma
TANZANIA
SEYCHELLES
Luanda
ANGOLA
COMOROS
ZAMBIA
MALAWI
Lilongwe
Lusaka
MADAGASCAR
Antananarivo
Harare
ZIM
MAURITIUS
NAMIBIA
BOTSWANA
MOZAMBIQUE
Réunion (France)
Windhoek
Gaborone
Pretoria
Maputo
Mbabane
SWAZILAND
Maseru
LESOTHO
REPUBLIC OF
SOUTH AFRICA

Bandar Seri Begawan
BR
Kuala Lumpur
MALAYSIA
SINGAPORE

I N D O N E S I A

Jakarta

EAST
TIMOR
Dili

PAPUA NEW
GUINEA
Port Moresby

SOLOMON
ISLANDS
Honiara

TUVALU

VANUATU
Port Vila

New
Caledonia
(France)

FIJI
Suva

I N D I A N

O C E A N

AUSTRALIA

Canberra

Tropic of Capricorn

**NEW
ZEALAND**
Wellington

☒ Kerguelen (France)

S O U T H E R N   O C E A N

Antarctic Circle

One centimetre on the map represents
1000 kilometres on the ground at the equator.

Arctic Circle

Svalbard
(Norway)

NGERIA

ANDORRA

FRANCE

Monaco

Malbord

ers

C T I C A

Europe   **Africa**   **Asia**   **Oceania**   **Antarctica**

You can see many features of the British Isles from space. The sea is shown as dark blue. Shallow water is light blue. Mountains are brown. Built-up areas are grey.

Ireland

Great Britain

There are two large islands and many smaller ones.

Shetland Islands

Lewis

Grampian Mountains

Glasgow

Lough Neagh

The Lake District

The Wash

Dublin

Birmingham

London

Brecon Beacons

Isles of Scilly

What other features can you name? **?**

Dartmoor

This map shows the height of the land, where the largest towns and cities are and how they are joined by motorways, major roads and main railway lines.

Key

- motorway
- major road
- main railway
- built-up area
- ⊡ largest towns
- ○ large towns
- • other towns
- land over 200m
- land between 200 and 500m
- land under 200m

Scale

One centimetre on the map represents 45 kilometres on the ground.

0   45   90   135km

The Great Glen is a Scottish valley so big it can be seen from space.

Shetland Islands

Orkney Islands

Cape Wrath

Thurso

Outer Hebrides

Lewis

NORTHWEST HIGHLANDS

Great Glen

Skye

Inverness

Loch Ness

River Spey

Cairngorms

River Dee

Aberdeen

1344m Ben Nevis

GRAMPIAN MOUNTAINS

Mull

R. Tay

Perth

Dundee

Loch Lomond

Firth of Forth

Islay

Glasgow

Edinburgh

R. Clyde

Ayr

SOUTHERN UPLANDS

River Tweed

Cheviot Hills

NORTH SEA

Londonderry

Antrim Mountains

Ballymena

Larne

R. Bann

Loch Neagh

Belfast

R. Erne

Sligo

Isle of Man

Stranraer

Carlisle

Lake District

978m Scafell Pike

PENNINES

R. Tees

Newcastle upon Tyne

Sunderland

Middlesbrough

North York Moors

Scarborough

Dundalk

852m Slieve Donard

R. Aire

York

Kingston upon Hull

IRISH SEA

Blackpool

Blackburn

Preston

Leeds

Bradford

Athlone

R. Shannon

Galway

Anglesey

Liverpool

Manchester

Sheffield

R. Trent

River Humber

Holyhead

Dublin

1085m Snowdon

Stoke-on-Trent

Nottingham

The Wash

CAMBRIAN MOUNTAINS

R. Dee

Derby

Leicester

The Fens

Norwich

Limerick

Wicklow Mountains

R. Barrow

Wolverhampton

Northampton

Peterborough

Tralee

1041m Carrantuohill

Cork

R. Blackwater

Waterford

Wexford

Rosslare

Fishguard

Brecon Beacons

Birmingham

R. Wye

R. Severn

R. Avon

Milton Keynes

Cambridge

Ipswich

Luton

ATLANTIC OCEAN

Cambrian Mountains

Cardigan Bay

St. George's Channel

Swansea

Newport

Cardiff

Bristol Channel

Exmoor

Cotswold Hills

Oxford

Chiltern Hills

R. Thames

Reading

London

Southend-on-Sea

Dover

North Downs

Salisbury Plain

South Downs

Folkestone

Strait of Dover

R. Exe

Dartmoor

Exeter

Weymouth

Poole

Bournemouth

Southampton

Portsmouth

Isle of Wight

Brighton

Plymouth

Land's End

Penzance

Isles of Scilly

English Channel

Channel Islands

North Channel

Firth of Clyde

Which places on the map have you heard about?

Which places on the map have you visited?

?

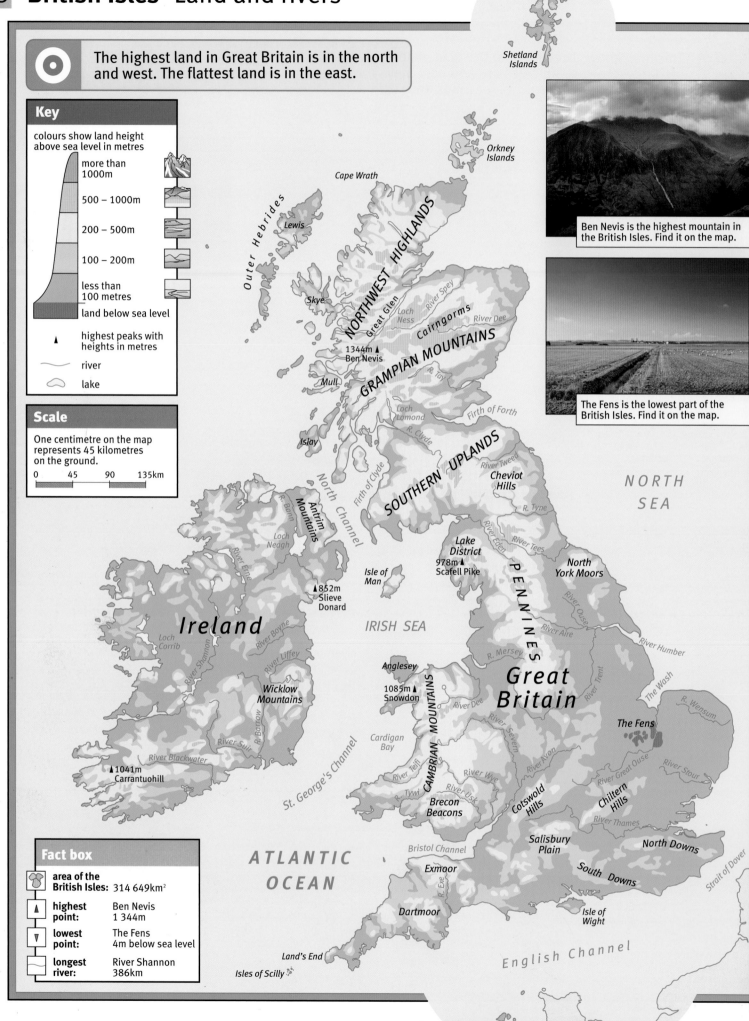

The highest land in Great Britain is in the north and west. The flattest land is in the east.

Key

colours show land height above sea level in metres

- more than 1000m
- 500 – 1000m
- 200 – 500m
- 100 – 200m
- less than 100 metres
- land below sea level

▲ highest peaks with heights in metres

⌇ river

lake

Scale

One centimetre on the map represents 45 kilometres on the ground.

0   45   90   135km

Fact box

area of the British Isles: 314 649km²

▲ highest point: Ben Nevis 1 344m

▼ lowest point: The Fens 4m below sea level

longest river: River Shannon 386km

Ben Nevis is the highest mountain in the British Isles. Find it on the map.

The Fens is the lowest part of the British Isles. Find it on the map.

Shetland Islands

Orkney Islands

Cape Wrath

Outer Hebrides

Lewis

NORTHWEST HIGHLANDS

Skye

Great Glen

Loch Ness

River Spey

Cairngorms

River Dee

1344m ▲ Ben Nevis

GRAMPIAN MOUNTAINS

Mull

R. Tay

Islay

Loch Lomond

Firth of Forth

R. Clyde

Firth of Clyde

SOUTHERN UPLANDS

River Tweed

Cheviot Hills

R. Tyne

NORTH SEA

North Channel

Antrim Mountains

Loch Neagh

River Bann

River Erne

Ireland

Loch Corrib

River Shannon

River Boyne

River Liffey

Wicklow Mountains

R. Barrow

River Suir

River Blackwater

▲1041m Carrantuohill

Isle of Man

▲852m Slieve Donard

IRISH SEA

Lake District

978m ▲ Scafell Pike

River Eden

River Tees

North York Moors

River Ouse

PENNINES

River Aire

River Mersey

River Humber

Anglesey

1085m ▲ Snowdon

CAMBRIAN MOUNTAINS

River Dee

River Trent

The Wash

R. Wensum

Cardigan Bay

River Severn

Great Britain

The Fens

River Great Ouse

River Stour

St. George's Channel

River Teifi

R. Tywi

River Wye

River Usk

River Avon

Cotswold Hills

Chiltern Hills

River Thames

North Downs

Brecon Beacons

Salisbury Plain

Bristol Channel

Exmoor

South Downs

ATLANTIC OCEAN

Dartmoor

R. Exe

Isle of Wight

Strait of Dover

Land's End

English Channel

Isles of Scilly

Channel Islands

In **summer,** the warmest part of the British Isles is the south coast. In **winter** the mountains of Scotland are the coldest parts.

It rains throughout the year. Western mountain areas are the wettest. Eastern areas are the driest.

Extreme rainfall in November 2009 caused flooding in Cumbria.

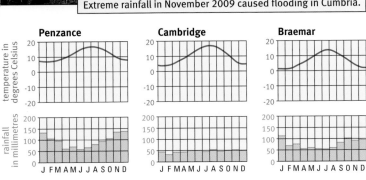

Penzance

Cambridge

Braemar

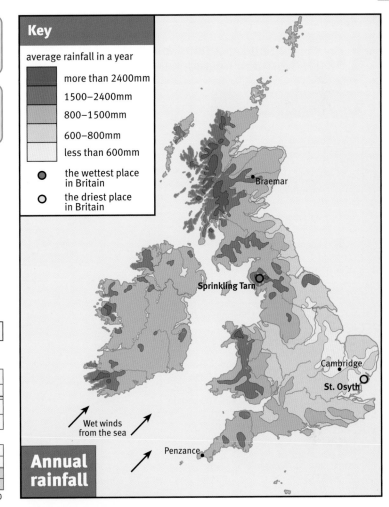

Key

average rainfall in a year

- more than 2400mm
- 1500–2400mm
- 800–1500mm
- 600–800mm
- less than 600mm
- ○ the wettest place in Britain
- ○ the driest place in Britain

Braemar

Sprinkling Tarn

Cambridge

St. Osyth

Wet winds from the sea

Penzance

Annual rainfall

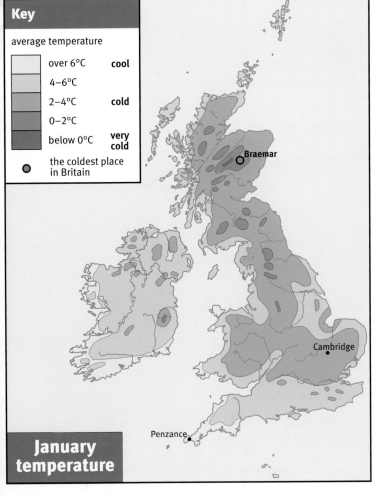

Key

average temperature

- over 6°C **cool**
- 4–6°C
- 2–4°C **cold**
- 0–2°C
- below 0°C **very cold**
- ○ the coldest place in Britain

Braemar

Cambridge

Penzance

January temperature

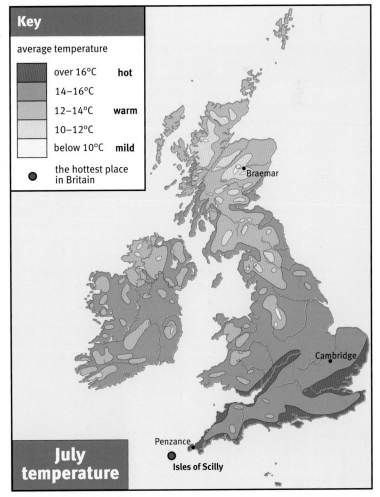

Key

average temperature

- over 16°C **hot**
- 14–16°C
- 12–14°C **warm**
- 10–12°C
- below 10°C **mild**
- ● the hottest place in Britain

Braemar

Cambridge

Penzance

Isles of Scilly

July temperature

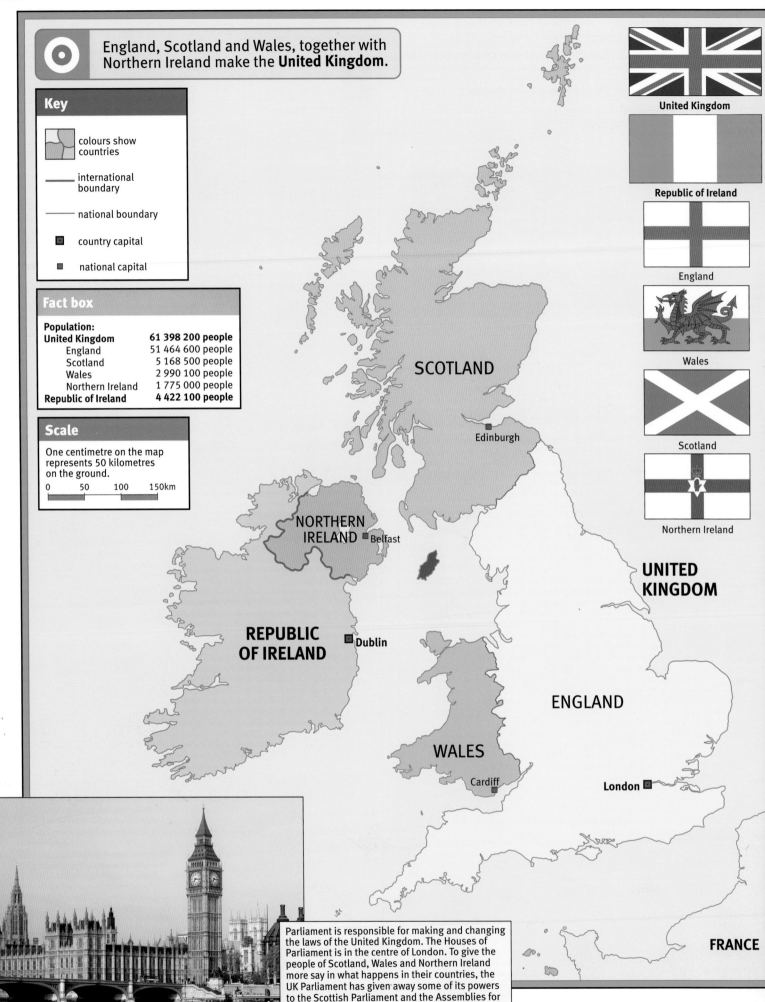

England, Scotland and Wales, together with Northern Ireland make the **United Kingdom**.

Key

colours show countries

international boundary

national boundary

■ country capital

■ national capital

Fact box

Population:
United Kingdom	**61 398 200 people**
England	51 464 600 people
Scotland	5 168 500 people
Wales	2 990 100 people
Northern Ireland	1 775 000 people
Republic of Ireland	**4 422 100 people**

Scale

One centimetre on the map represents 50 kilometres on the ground.

0   50   100   150km

United Kingdom

Republic of Ireland

England

Wales

Scotland

Northern Ireland

SCOTLAND

Edinburgh

NORTHERN IRELAND ■ Belfast

REPUBLIC OF IRELAND ■ Dublin

UNITED KINGDOM

ENGLAND

WALES

Cardiff

London ■

FRANCE

Parliament is responsible for making and changing the laws of the United Kingdom. The Houses of Parliament is in the centre of London. To give the people of Scotland, Wales and Northern Ireland more say in what happens in their countries, the UK Parliament has given away some of its powers to the Scottish Parliament and the Assemblies for Wales and Northern Ireland.

The European Union (EU) was set up in 1957 so that its people could live in peace and have a better quality of life. Since then it has grown from six member countries to twenty-seven. Other countries hope to join.

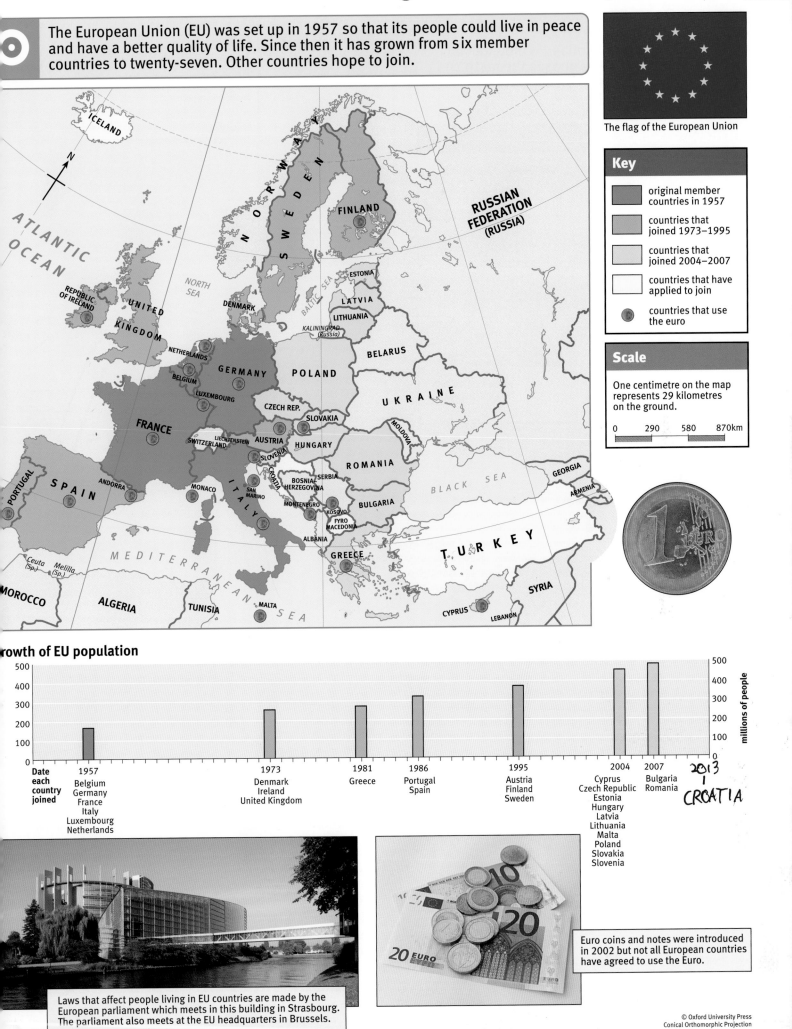

The flag of the European Union

Key

- original member countries in 1957
- countries that joined 1973–1995
- countries that joined 2004–2007
- countries that have applied to join
- countries that use the euro

Scale

One centimetre on the map represents 29 kilometres on the ground.

0   290   580   870km

Growth of EU population

millions of people

Date each country joined	1957	1973	1981	1986	1995	2004	2007	2013
	Belgium Germany France Italy Luxembourg Netherlands	Denmark Ireland United Kingdom	Greece	Portugal Spain	Austria Finland Sweden	Cyprus Czech Republic Estonia Hungary Latvia Lithuania Malta Poland Slovakia Slovenia	Bulgaria Romania	CROATIA

Laws that affect people living in EU countries are made by the European parliament which meets in this building in Strasbourg. The parliament also meets at the EU headquarters in Brussels.

Euro coins and notes were introduced in 2002 but not all European countries have agreed to use the Euro.

© Oxford University Press
Conical Orthomorphic Projection

Northern Scotland is mountainous with many islands to the north and west. Its spectacular scenery brings many visitors.

Locator

Scale

One centimetre on the map represents 12.5 kilometres on the ground.

0   12.5   25   37.5km

Key

▬▬▬	international boundary
▬ ▬ ▬	national boundary
═══	motorway
▬▬▬	main road
▬▬▬	railway
⊕	main airport
∿	river
┉┉	canal
◠	lake

land height

above sea level in metres

more than 1000m

500 – 1000m

200 – 500m

100 – 200m

less than 100 metres

land below sea level

▲ highest peaks with heights in metres

towns

◭	built-up area
⊡	largest towns
○	large towns
•	other towns

5°W

59°N

6°W

ATLANTIC OCEAN

Outer Hebrides

St. Kilda

Scarp

Taransay

Pabbay
Berneray

North Uist

Benbecula

South Uist

Lochboisdale

Eriskay

Barra

Vatersay   Castlebay

Mingulay

8°W   7°W

Butt of Lewis   Port of Ness

Lewis

Broad Bay

Eye Peninsula

Stornoway

Loch Langavat

Clisham 799m ▲

Tarbert

Harris

Scalpay

Shiant

Sound of Harris

Little Minch

Rubha Hunish

Kilmaluag

Loch Snizort

Uig

The Storr 719m ▲

Dunvegan

Portree

Cuillin Hills

Skye

Soay

Canna

Kinloch

Rhum

Eigg

Muck

Sound of Arisaig

Inner Hebrides

Lochmaddy

58°N

57°N

Cape Wrath   Durness

Eddrachillis Bay

927m ▲ Ben Hope

961m ▲ Be Klibrec

Lochinver

Enard Bay

998m ▲ Ben More Assynt

Loch Broom

Ullapool

Beinn Dearg 1081m ▲

Ben Wyvis 1046m

1109m ▲ Sgurr Mór

Loch Fannich

Poolewe

Gairloch

Loch Maree

Loch Torridon

NORTHWEST HIGHLANDS

Dingwa

Conon Bridge

Muir of Ord

The Minch

Kyle of Lochalsh

Scalpay

Broadford

Calligarry

Sound of Sleat

Mallaig

Arisaig

Loch Morar

Loch Shiel

Fort William

Ben Nevis ▲ 1344m

Sound of Raasay

Inner Sound

Raasay

Carn Eige 1183m ▲

Loch Monar

SCO

Drumnadrochit

Loch Ness

Invermoriston

Fort Augustus

Invergarry

Loch Garry

Loch Arkaig

Loch Lochy

Orrin Reservoir

Loch Laggan

Lai

Br

6°W

© Oxford University Press
Transverse Mercator Projection

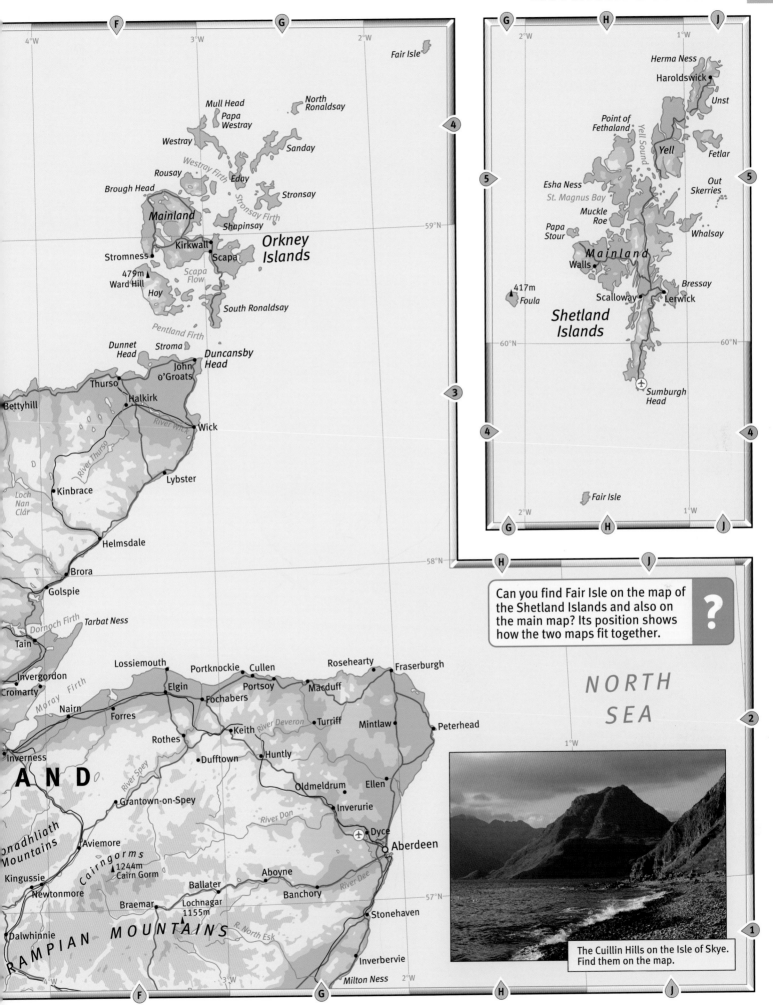

F · **G**

4°W · 3°W · 2°W

Fair Isle

Mull Head
Papa
Westray

North
Ronaldsay

Westray

Sanday

Rousay
Brough Head

Westray Firth

Eday

Stronsay

Stronsay Firth

Mainland

Shapinsay

59°N

Kirkwall
Stromness
Scapa

**Orkney
Islands**

479m ▲
Ward Hill

*Scapa
Flow*

Hoy

South Ronaldsay

Pentland Firth

Dunnet
Head

Stroma

Duncansby
Head

John
o'Groats

Thurso
Halkirk

Bettyhill

River Wick

Wick

River Thurso

Lybster

Kinbrace

Helmsdale

Brora

58°N

Golspie

Dornoch Firth
Tarbat Ness

*Loch
Nan
Clár*

Tain

Invergordon

Cromarty

Moray Firth

Nairn

Lossiemouth
Portknockie
Cullen
Rosehearty
Fraserburgh

Elgin
Portsoy
Macduff

Forres
Fochabers

River Deveron
Turriff

Rothes
Keith

Mintlaw
Peterhead

Inverness

Huntly

Dufftown

Oldmeldrum
Ellen

Grantown-on-Spey

Inverurie

River Spey

River Don

onadhliath
Mountains

Dyce

Aviemore

Cairngorms

Aberdeen

Kingussie

1244m
Cairn Gorm

Aboyne

Newtonmore

Ballater

River Dee

Braemar
Lochnagar
1155m

Banchory

57°N

Dalwhinnie

RAMPIAN MOUNTAINS

R. North Esk

Stonehaven

Inverbervie

Milton Ness

F · **G**

4°W · 3°W · 2°W

G · **H** · **J**

2°W · 1°W

Herma Ness
Haroldswick

Unst

Point of
Fethaland

4

Yell

Fetlar

Yell Sound

Esha Ness

5

Out
Skerries

St. Magnus Bay

Muckle
Roe

Papa
Stour

Walls

Mainland

Whalsay

417m ▲
Foula

Scalloway

Bressay

Lerwick

60°N

**Shetland
Islands**

Sumburgh
Head

4

Fair Isle

G · **H** · **J**

2°W · 1°W

H · **J**

Can you find Fair Isle on the map of
the Shetland Islands and also on
the main map? Its position shows
how the two maps fit together. **?**

**NORTH
SEA**

1°W

2

1

The Cuillin Hills on the Isle of Skye.
Find them on the map.

© Oxford University Press

In the centre of Northern Ireland lies Lough Neagh, the largest lake in the British Isles.

Locator

On the north coast of Northern Ireland, black basalt rock forms the Giant's Causeway. Find it on the map.

A B C D

3

2

1

7°W
8°W
6°W
5°W

56°N
55°N
54°N

Muck
Coll
Tiree
Tobermory
Lochaline
Ulva
Craignure
Lismore
Iona
967m Ben More
Mull
Fionnphort
Ross of Mull
Kerrera
Oban
Ben Cruachan 1124m
Scarba
Colonsay
Scalasaig
Oronsay
Loch Awe
Loch Etive
Loch Linnhe
Sound of Mull
Loch Shiel
Fort William
1344m Ben Nevis
Blackwater Reservoir
Kinlochleven
GRAMPIAN MOUNTAINS
Loch Rannoch
Ben Lawers 1214m
Loch Lyon
River Orchy
Tyndrum
Crianlarich
Ben More 1174m
Lochearn
Loch Ea
SCOTLAND
Inveraray
974m Ben Lomond
Calla
River For
Furnace
Strachur
Loch Lomond
Lochgilphead
Loch Long
Garelochhead
River Fore
Jura
Helensburgh
Campsie Fell
Sound of Jura
Loch Fyne
Dunoon
Greenock
Port Glasgow
Dumbarton
Kirkintillo
Clydebank
Bearsden
Coatb
Port Askaig
Craighouse
Tarbert
Rothesay
Johnstone
Paisley
Glas
Kennacraig
Bute
Largs
Barrhead
Hamilt
Islay
Clachan
Newton Mearns
East Kilbr
Gigha
Lochranza
Goat Fell 874m
Ardrossan
Stewarton
Portnahaven
Kintyre
Saltcoats
Irvine
Darvel
Mull of Oa
Port Ellen
Kilbrannan Sound
Brodick
Arran
Kilmarnock
River Ayr
Prestwick
Ayr
Campbeltown
Sound of Bute
Firth of Clyde
Maybole
New Cumnock
Mull of Kintyre
Southend
Ailsa Craig
River Doon
Girvan
Cumno
SOUTHER
North Channel
Ballantrae
New Galloway
Malin Head
Lough Swilly
Inishowen Peninsula
615m Slieve Snaght
Lough Foyle
Rathlin Island
Rathlin Sound
Fair Head
Corsewall Point
Newton Stewart
Creeslough
Buncrana
Portrush
Giant's Causeway
Bushmills
Ballycastle
Cairnryan
Stranraer
Wigtown
Gatehouse of Fleet
Coleraine
Ballymoney
R. Bush
Kilmacrenan
Lough Foyle
Limavady
Antrim Mountains
Kirkcudbri
Letterkenny
Londonderry
Dungiven
River Bann
Carnlough
Glenluce
River Foyle
Ballybofey
Lifford
Strabane
Maghera
R. Main
Ballymena
Larne
Island Magee
Drummore
Whithorn
R. Finn
Sperrin Mountains
683m Sawel
Magherafelt
Randalstown
Mull of Galloway
R. Derg
Newtownstewart
Antrim
Carrickfergus
Donegal
NORTHERN IRELAND
Omagh
Cookstown
Lough Neagh
Newtownabbey
Crumlin
Belfast
Bangor
Donaghadee
Point of Ay
Lough Derg
Coalisland
Newtownards
Lisburn
Ards Peninsula
Ramsey
Irvinestown
Dungannon
Lurgan
Saintfield
Snaefell 620m
Lower Lough Erne
Aughnacloy
Portadown
Craigavon
Dromore
Strangford Lough
Kirk Michael
Manorhamilton
Enniskillen
R. Blackwater
Armagh
R. Logan
Peel
Isle of Man
Banbridge
River Bann
Downpatrick
Monaghan
Keady
Upper Lough Erne
Lisnaskea
Newtownhamilton
Newcastle
St. John's Point
Douglas
Clones
Newry
852m Slieve Donard
Port Erin
Castleblayney
Warrenpoint
Mourne Mtns.
Calf of Man
Castletown
Cavan
Crossmaglen
Kilkeel
R. Shannon

Most Scottish people live in the lowlands between Glasgow and Edinburgh.

Scale

One centimetre on the map represents 12.5 kilometres on the ground.

0   12.5   25   37.5km

Key

▬▬▬	international boundary
- - -	national boundary
───	motorway
───	main road
───	railway
⊕	main airport
∿	river
───	canal
◠	lake

towns

- ⬠ built-up area
- ⊡ largest towns
- ○ large towns
- • other towns

land height

above sea level in metres

	more than 1000m
	500 – 1000m
	200 – 500m
	100 – 200m
	less than 100 metres
	land below sea level
▲	highest peaks with heights in metres

Can you name five lakes in the English Lake District? **?**

NORTH SEA

E N G L A N D

Map labels:

Pitlochry, Aberfeldy, Kirriemuir, Blairgowrie, Brechin, Inverbervie, Milton Ness, Montrose, Forfar, Arbroath, Carnoustie, Sidlaw Hills, R. South Esk, Crieff, Perth, Dundee, Leuchars, St. Andrews, Auchterarder, Cupar, River Earn, Auchtermuchty, Anstruther, River Tay, Ochil Hills, Kinross, Glenrothes, Loch Leven, Tillicoultry, Buckhaven, Cowdenbeath, Kirkcaldy, Alloa, Dunfermline, North Berwick, Grangemouth, Inverkeithing, Dunbar, Firth of Forth, Firth of Tay, Falkirk, bernauld, Linlithgow, Edinburgh, Haddington, St. Abb's Head, Bathgate, Livingston, Musselburgh, Eyemouth, drie, Dalkeith, Lammermuir Hills, erwell, Penicuik, Berwick-upon-Tweed, ishaw, Pentland Hills, Duns, Holy Island, Lanark, Peebles, Coldstream, Bamburgh, Biggar, Galashiels, River Tweed, Broad Law 840m, Melrose, Kelso, Selkirk, Wooler, The Cheviot 815m, quhar, Daer Reservoir, R. Teviot, Jedburgh, Alnwick, Moffat, Hawick, Ettrick Water, River Esk, R. Aln, rnhill, Peel Fell 602m, Amble, Cheviot Hills, River Coquet, Langholm, Kielder Water, Ashington, Lockerbie, Liddell Water, R. North Tyne, R. Wansbeck, Dumfries, Blyth, Cramlington, Whitley Bay, Tynemouth, Newcastle upon Tyne, South Shields, Annan, R. Irthing, Gateshead, stle, Haltwhistle, Hexham, R. Tyne, Sunderland, uglas, Dalbeattie, Brampton, Consett, Washington, Houghton-le-Spring, Solway Firth, Chester-le-Street, Carlisle, River Eden, Peterlee, Wigton, PENNINES, Durham, Cross Fell 893m, River Wear, Spennymoor, Hartlepool, Maryport, Bishop Auckland, Billingham, Redcar, Skiddaw 931m, Penrith, Mickle Fell 790m, Newton Aycliffe, Stockton-on-Tees, Workington, Cockermouth, Derwent Water, Ullswater, Middlesbrough, Helvellyn 950m, Barnard Castle, Darlington, Thornaby-on-Tees, Guisborough, Whitehaven, Keswick, Appleby-in-Westmorland, Brough, R. Tees, Whitby, St. Bees Head, Cleveland Hills, River Esk, Scafell Pike 978m, Lake District, Richmond, North York Moors, Seascale, Ambleside, Windermere, Northallerton, Scarborough, Wast Water, River Swale, Pickering, Kendal, Leyburn, Thirsk, Filey, Coniston Water, Whernside 737m, River Ure, Vale of Pickering, Ulverston, River Lune, Great Whernside 704m, Malton, Ripon, Yorkshire Wolds, Barrow-in-Furness, Carnforth, Ingleborough 723m, 693m Pen-y-Ghent, Bridlington, Morecambe, Lancaster, Settle, River Nidd, Haxby, Great Driffield, Heysham, Ward's Stone 560m, R. Wharfe, River Aire, Knaresborough, York, Pocklington, Hornsea, Harrogate

Most of Wales is mountainous. The largest towns and cities are in the south.

Wales is wet. Can you name two Welsh reservoirs? **?**

IRISH SEA

Isle of Man
Port Erin
Calf of Man
Castletown

Barrow-in-Furness
Morecambe
Carnforth
Lancaster
Heysham
Fleetwood
Thornton
Blackpool
Preston
Lytham St. Anne's
Blac
Leyland
Darw
Ch
Southport
Formby
Skelmersdale
Wigan
Bootle
Kirkby
St. Helens
Wallasey
Birkenhead
Liverpool
Widnes
Warr
Runcorn
Ellesmere Port
Nort
Winsford
Chester
Wrexham
Nantwich
Ruabon
Whit
Mar
Dray
Oswestry
Shrewsbury
Welling
Tel
Welshpool
40
The Wre
Montgomery
Wenlock Edge
54
Newtown
Br
Cle
Llanidloes
Ludlow
Knighton
Leomins
Llandrindod Wells
Kington
Builth Wells
Hay-on-Wye
Herefor
Ross-on-Wye
Cinde

Balbriggan

Swords
Dublin
Dún Laoghaire
Bray

Wicklow

Arklow

Cahore Point

Carmel Head
Amlwch
Holyhead
Anglesey
Holy Island
Llangefni
Menai Bridge
Bangor
Bethesda
Caernarfon
Caernarfon Bay
Snowdon 1085m
Conwy
Llandudno
Rhyl
Prestatyn
Colwyn Bay
Holywell
Denbigh
Connah's Quay
Flint
Llanrwst
Mold
Betws-y-Coed
Ruthin
Llyn Brenig
River Dee
River Dee
R. Mersey

Lleyn Peninsula
Porthmadog
Blaenau Ffestiniog
Corwen
Llangollen
Pwllheli
Harlech
Bala
Bala Lake
Chirk
Llyn Vyrnwy
R. Dee
R. Vyrnwy

Bardsey Island
Dolgellau
Barmouth
892m Cadair Idris
Machynlleth
R. Dyfi
R. Severn

Cardigan Bay
Tywyn
Plynlimon 752m
Newtown
Aberystwyth
Llanidloes
WALES

Aberaeron
New Quay
Rhayader
Claerwen Reservoir
Llandrindod Wells
Llyn Brianne Reservoir
Builth Wells
R. Wye
Cemaes Head
Cardigan
Lampeter
Mynydd Eppynt
Hay-on-Wye
St. George's Channel
Strumble Head
Newport
River Teifi
Black Mountains
Newcastle Emlyn
Fishguard
St. David's Head
Preseli Mountains
Llandovery
Brecon
St. Brides Bay
Carmarthen
Llandeilo
R. Tywi
River Usk
886m
Abergavenny
Monmouth
St. Clears
Brecon Beacons
Milford Haven
Cross Hands
Ammanford
Merthyr Tydfil
Tredegar
Ebbw Vale
Abertillery
R. Neath
Aberdare
Mountain Ash
Pontypool
Cwmbran
Saundersfoot
Kidwelly
Pembroke Dock
Tenby
Burry Port
Llanelli
Pontardulais
Rhondda
Gelligaer
Chepstow
Pembroke
Gorseinon
Neath
Pontypridd
Caerphilly
Newport
Carmarthen Bay
Swansea
Maesteg
Gower
Port Talbot
Worms Head
Porthcawl
Bridgend
Cardiff
Mangotsfield
Barry
Clevedon
Bristol
Penarth
Kingsw
Bristol Channel
Weston-super-Mare
Keyns

The Millennium Stadium, Cardiff. Find Cardiff on the map.

CAMBRIAN MOUNTAINS

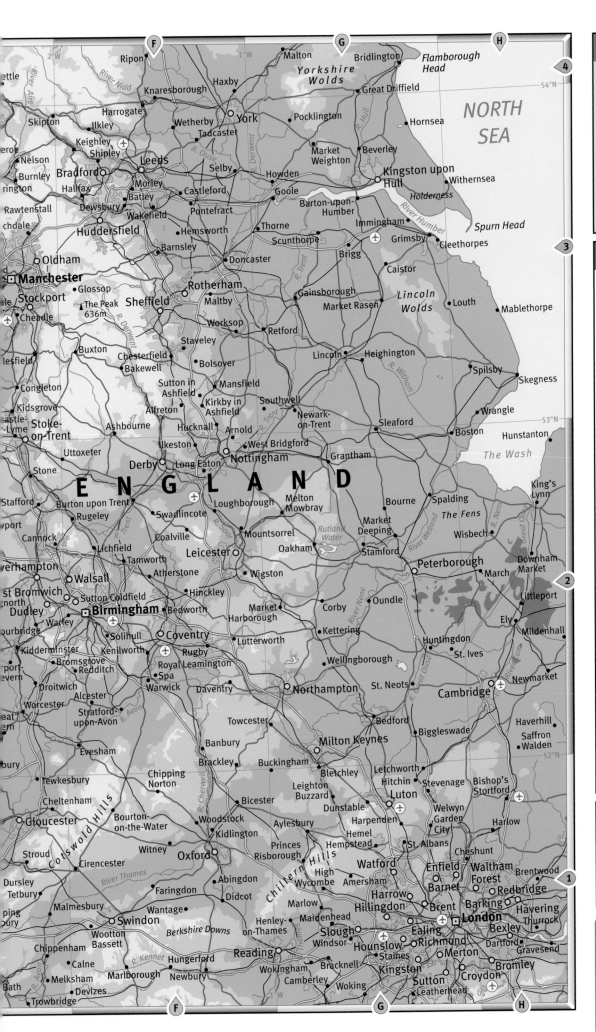

NORTH SEA

Locator

Key

———	international boundary
– – –	national boundary
	motorway
	main road
	railway
⊕	main airport
	river
	canal
	lake

towns

	built-up area
⊡	largest towns
○	large towns
•	other towns

land height

above sea level in metres

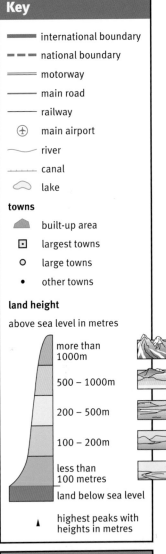

	more than 1000m
	500 – 1000m
	200 – 500m
	100 – 200m
	less than 100 metres
	land below sea level
▲	highest peaks with heights in metres

Scale

One centimetre on the map represents 12.5 kilometres on the ground.

0   12.5   25   37.5km

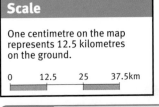

Many towns and cities in England have grown together to make large built-up areas called **conurbations**.

© Oxford University Press

Locator

Key

- ━━━ international boundary
- ╌╌╌ national boundary
- ═══ motorway
- ─── main road
- ─── railway
- ⊕ main airport
- ～ river
- ┼┼┼ canal
- ～ lake

towns
- ⬠ built-up area
- ⊡ largest towns
- ○ large towns
- • other towns

land height

above sea level in metres

- more than 1000m
- 500 – 1000m
- 200 – 500m
- 100 – 200m
- less than 100 metres
- land below sea level
- ▲ highest peaks with heights in metres

Scale

One centimetre on the map represents 12.5 kilometres on the ground.

0   12.5   25   37.5km

Can you name the water between the Isle of Wight and the mainland? **?**

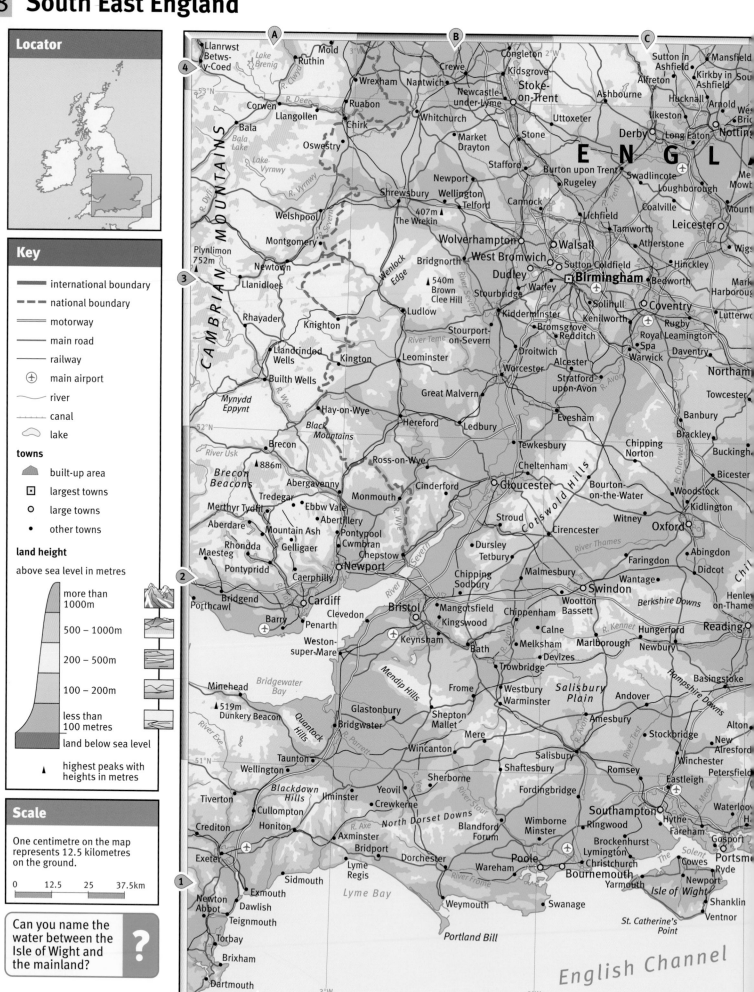

NORTH SEA

Spilsby
Skegness
Wrangle
Sleaford
Boston
Grantham
Hunstanton
Wells-next-the-Sea
Cromer
The Wash
Fakenham
North Walsham
Bourne
Spalding
Aylsham
Market Deeping
The Fens
King's Lynn
Norwich
Acle
Great Yarmouth
Wisbech
Swaffham
East Dereham
Stamford
Peterborough
Downham Market
Wymondham
Lowestoft
March
Attleborough
Bungay
Beccles
Corby
Oundle
Littleport
Thetford
Diss
Kettering
Ely
Mildenhall
Southwold
Wellingborough
Huntingdon
St. Ives
Saxmundham
St. Neots
Newmarket
Bury St. Edmunds
Stowmarket
Wickham Market
Aldeburgh
Cambridge
Haverhill
Woodbridge
Bedford
Sudbury
Ipswich
Biggleswade
Saffron Walden
Felixstowe
Milton Keynes
Harwich
Bletchley
Letchworth
Hitchin
Stevenage
Bishop's Stortford
Braintree
Walton-on-the-Naze
Leighton Buzzard
Luton
Welwyn Garden City
Harlow
Witham
Colchester
Dunstable
Harpenden
Clacton-on-Sea
Hemel Hempstead
St. Albans
Chelmsford
Watford
Cheshunt
Brentwood
Southminster
Enfield
Waltham Forest
Rayleigh
Amersham
Barnet
Redbridge
Basildon
Harrow
Brent
Barking
Hillingdon
Havering
Southend-on-Sea
London
Ealing
Bexley
Thurrock
Sheerness
Richmond
Dartford
Gravesend
Herne Bay
Margate
Hounslow
Merton
Chatham
North Foreland
Staines
Bromley
Gillingham
Whitstable
Ramsgate
Kingston
Croydon
Sittingbourne
Canterbury
Woking
Sutton
Leatherhead
Sevenoaks
Maidstone
Deal
Farnborough
Reigate
Tonbridge
North Downs
Guildford
Redhill
Ashford
Dover
Godalming
Dorking
Royal Tunbridge Wells
Folkestone
Haslemere
East Grinstead
Hythe
Crawley
Crowborough
New Romney
Midhurst
Horsham
Uckfield
Rye
Billingshurst
Haywards Heath
Dungeness
Littlehampton
Lewes
Hailsham
Hastings
Bognor Regis
Hove
Brighton
Bexhill
Worthing
Seaford
Eastbourne
Beachy Head
South Downs

R. Witham
R. Nene
River Welland
Rutland Water
River Nene
River Waveney
River Wensum
River Bure
Great Ouse
R. Cam
River Stour
River Colne
R. Medway
R. Arun
Strait of Dover

FRANCE
BELGIUM
Nieuwpoort
Veurne
Dunkerque
Calais
Ardres
Cassel
St-Omer
Hazebrouck
Boulogne-sur-Mer
Lillers
Béthune
Le Touquet-Paris-Plage

53°N
52°N
51°N
1°E
2°E
0°

Eastern England is mostly low and flat. Some land is below sea level.

Brighton is one of Britain's oldest seaside resorts. Find it on the map.

Can you name the nearest French city to England?

South west England is a long peninsula with a rocky coastline.

Milford Haven
Pembroke Dock
Pembroke
Saundersfoot
Tenby
Burry Port
Llanelli
Carmarthen Bay
Gorseinon
Gower
Worms Head
Cross Hands
Kidwelly
Pontardulais
Neath
Maesteg
Swansea
Port Talbot
Porthcawl
Bridgend
Barry

Ammanford
Aberdare
Merthyr Tydfil
Mountain Ash
Rhondda
Pontypridd
Abergavenny
Tredegar
Abertillery
Ebbw Val
Gelligaer
Caerphilly
Newport
Cardif
Penarth
Weston-super-Mare

Bristol Channel

Bridgewater Bay

Lundy
Ilfracombe
Croyde
Hartland Point
Lynton
Exmoor
Minehead
519m
▲
Dunkery Beacon
Quantock Hills
Bridgw

Barnstable or Bideford Bay
Barnstaple
South Molton
Bideford
Great Torrington
Chulmleigh
Tiverton
Wellington
Taunton
Blackdown Hills
Ilm

Bude
Bude Bay
Holsworthy
Hatherleigh
Okehampton
Crediton
Cullompton
Honiton
Axminster

Boscastle
Brown Willy 420m ▲
Launceston
Yes Tor 619m ▲
River Teign
Dartmoor
Exeter
Sidmouth

Trevose Head
Padstow
Wadebridge
Bodmin
Bodmin Moor
Callington
Tavistock
Newton Abbot
Exmouth
Dawlish
Teignmouth

Newquay
St. Agnes
Truro
Redruth
St. Ives
Camborne
Hayle
Penzance
Helston
Land's End
Mount's Bay

St. Austell
Lostwithiel
Fowey
Looe
Saltash
Plymouth
Ashburton
Buckfastleigh
Totnes
Torbay
Brixham
Dartmouth
Kingsbridge
Salcombe
Start Point
Bigbury Bay

Falmouth

Lizard
Lizard Point

Tresco
St. Mary's
Isles of Scilly

Land's End is the most south westerly tip of mainland Great Britain. Find it on the map.

Locator

Key

————	international boundary
- - - -	national boundary
══════	motorway
————	main road
————	railway
⊕	main airport
～	river
··········	canal
⌒	lake

towns

◥	built-up area
▣	largest towns
○	large towns
•	other towns

land height

above sea level in metres

more than 1000m	
500 – 1000m	
200 – 500m	
100 – 200m	
less than 100 metres	
land below sea level	

▲ highest peaks with heights in metres

Scale

One centimetre on the map represents 12.5 kilometres on the ground.

0   12.5   25   37.5km

Are the Channel Islands nearer to England or to France? **?**

Map labels

Cinderford, Stroud, Cirencester, Witney, Oxford, Kidlington, Aylesbury, Princes Risborough, Hemel Hempstead, St. Albans, Cheshunt, Watford, Enfield, Barnet, Brent, London, Harrow, Hillingdon, Amersham, High Wycombe, Marlow, Maidenhead, Slough, Windsor, Hounslow, Ealing, Richmond, Merton, Staines, Sutton, Kingston, Leatherhead, Reigate, Redhill, Dorking, Guildford, Godalming, Crawley, Horsham, Haslemere, Haywards Heath, Billingshurst, Hove, Brighton, Worthing, Littlehampton, Bognor Regis, Chichester, Selsey Bill

Dursley, Tetbury, Chipping Sodbury, Malmesbury, Faringdon, Abingdon, Didcot, Wantage, Swindon, Wootton Bassett, Berkshire Downs, Henley-on-Thames, Reading, Chippenham, Calne, Hungerford, Newbury, Wokingham, Bracknell, Camberley, Woking, Farnborough, Aldershot, Farnham, Basingstoke, Alton, Hindhead, Petersfield, Midhurst, South Downs, North Downs

Bristol, Mangotsfield, Kingswood, Keynsham, Bath, Melksham, Devizes, Marlborough, Trowbridge, Westbury, Warminster, Salisbury Plain, Andover, Stockbridge, New Alresford, Winchester, Waterlooville, Havant, Gosport, Portsmouth, Ryde

Frome, Shepton Mallet, Mendip Hills, Wincanton, Mere, Salisbury, Shaftesbury, Romsey, Eastleigh, Southampton, Hythe, Fareham, Cowes, Newport, Shanklin, Ventnor, Isle of Wight

ENGLAND, Sherborne, North Dorset Downs, Blandford Forum, Wimborne Minster, Ringwood, Brockenhurst, Lymington, Christchurch, Bournemouth, Yarmouth, St. Catherine's Point, Fordingbridge

Dorchester, Wareham, Poole, Swanage, Weymouth, Portland Bill, River Frome

English Channel, 50°N

Alderney, Auderville, Cap de la Hague, Barfleur, Cherbourg, Valognes, Baie de la Seine

Guernsey, Herm, St. Peter Port, Sark, Channel Islands, Carteret, Carentan, Bayeux, FRANCE, Lessay, Coutances, St-Lô, Caen, Jersey, St. John, St. Helier

The most crowded part of the United Kingdom is between London and Manchester.

Key

Population density

- very crowded
- quite crowded
- quite empty

Cities and towns
numbers of people

- ☐ more than 1 000 000
- ○ 400 000 – 1 000 000
- ◉ 100 000 – 400 000
- • 25 000 – 100 000

Scale

One centimetre on the map represents 45 kilometres on the ground.

0   45   90   135km

How many people live in the UK?

England	51.5 million
Scotland	5.2 million
Wales	3.0 million
N. Ireland	1.8 million
UK total	**61.4 million**

Where people live

If there were 100 people in the United Kingdom, this is where they would live:

- England
- Scotland
- Wales
- Northern Ireland

Population pyramid

If there were 100 people in the United Kingdom, this is how old they would be:

- over 90
- 80–89
- 70–79
- 60–69
- 50–59
- 40–49
- 30–39
- 20–29
- 10–19
- under 10

Population density
The number of people that live in an area

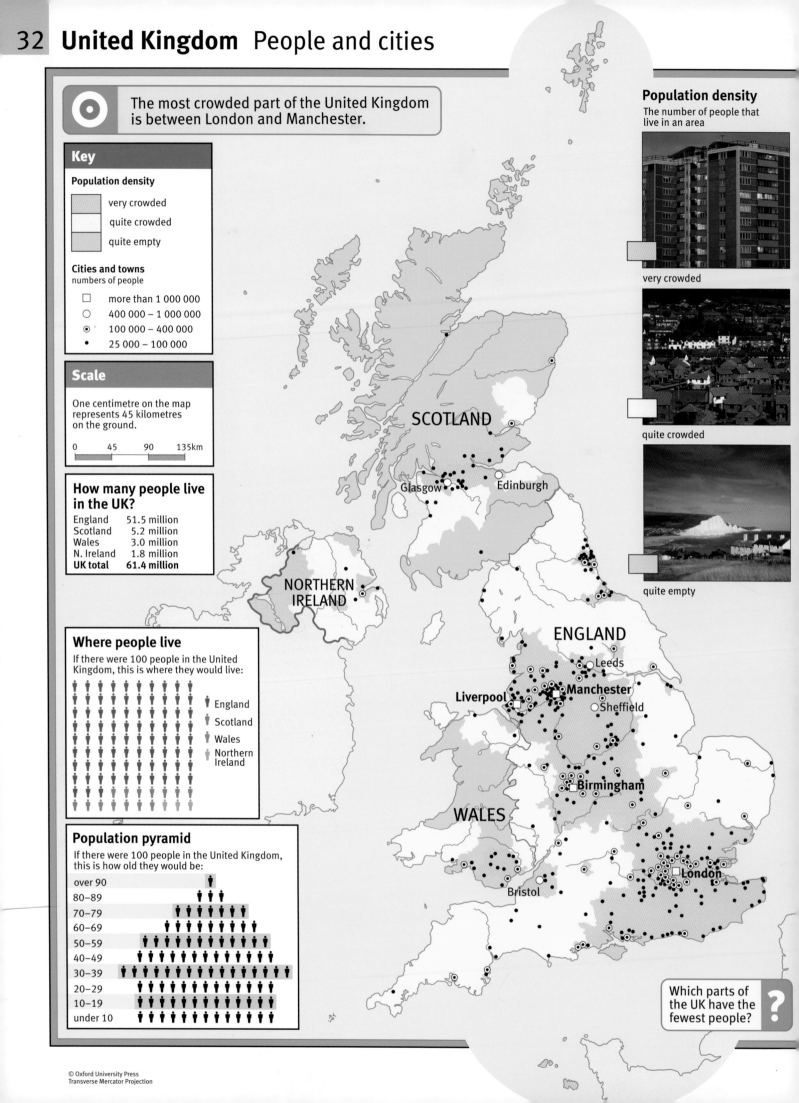

very crowded

quite crowded

quite empty

SCOTLAND

Glasgow   Edinburgh

NORTHERN IRELAND

ENGLAND

Leeds

Liverpool   Manchester

Sheffield

Birmingham

WALES

London

Bristol

Which parts of the UK have the fewest people?

Coal, oil and natural gas are **fossil fuels**. They cannot be replaced. Energy from wind and water is **renewable**. These sources of energy can be used again and again.

Key

- ■ largest coal mines
- ┅╫┅ gas field and pipeline
- ┅╫┅ oil field and pipeline

Largest power stations
- ● burning coal, oil or gas
- ● using water power
- ● using nuclear power
- ● using wind power

Scale

One centimetre on the map represents 50 kilometres on the ground.

0   50   100   150km

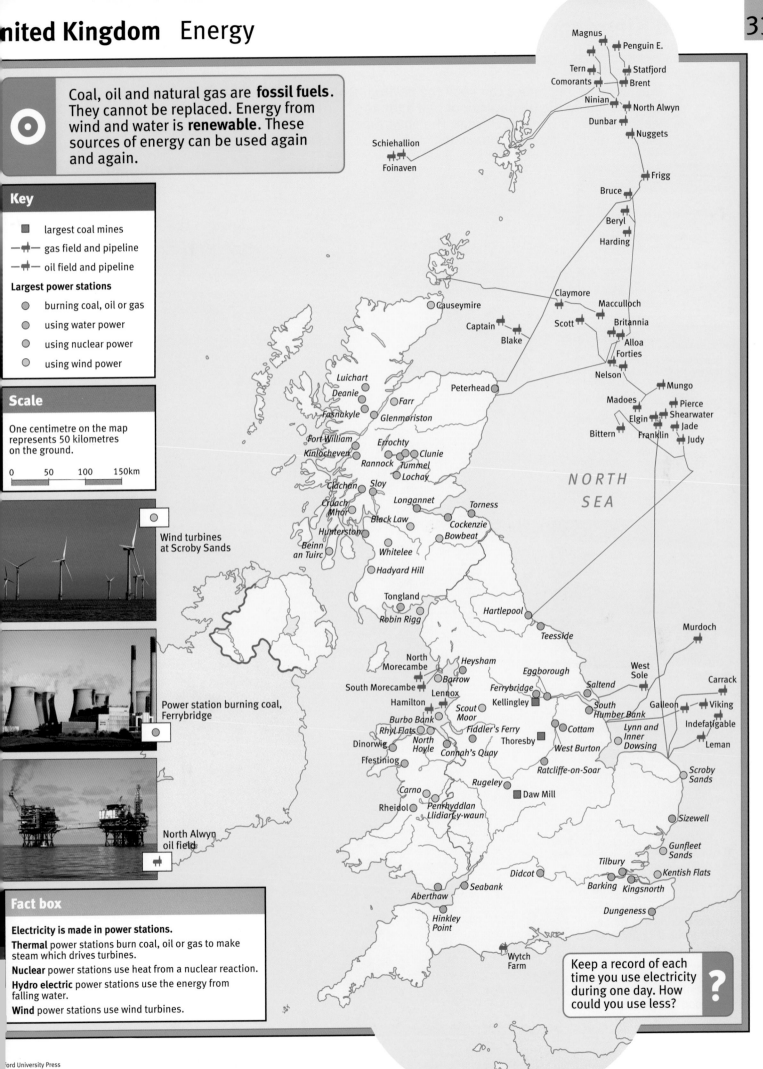

Wind turbines at Scroby Sands

Power station burning coal, Ferrybridge

North Alwyn oil field

Fact box

Electricity is made in power stations.

Thermal power stations burn coal, oil or gas to make steam which drives turbines.

Nuclear power stations use heat from a nuclear reaction.

Hydro electric power stations use the energy from falling water.

Wind power stations use wind turbines.

NORTH SEA

Keep a record of each time you use electricity during one day. How could you use less?

Magnus
Penguin E.
Tern
Statfjord
Comorants
Brent
Ninian
North Alwyn
Dunbar
Nuggets
Schiehallion
Foinaven
Frigg
Bruce
Beryl
Harding
Causeymire
Claymore
Macculloch
Captain
Scott
Britannia
Blake
Alloa
Forties
Luichart
Nelson
Deanie
Farr
Mungo
Peterhead
Madoes
Pierce
Fasnakyle
Glenmøriston
Shearwater
Elgin
Jade
Fort William
Errochty
Bittern
Franklin
Judy
Kinlocheven
Clunie
Rannock
Tummel
Lochay
Clachan
Sloy
Cruach
Longannet
Torness
Mhor
Huntertson
Black Law
Cockenzie
Beinn
Bowbeat
an Tuirc
Whitelee
Hadyard Hill
Tongland
Hartlepool
Murdoch
Robin Rigg
Teesside
North
Heysham
West
Sole
Morecambe
Carrack
South Morecambe
Barrow
Eggborough
Saltend
Galleon
Viking
Ferrybridge
Hamilton
Lennox
Kellingley
South
Indefatigable
Burbo Bank
Scout
Humber Bank
Rhyl Flats
Moor
Cottam
Lynn and
Leman
Dinorwig
North
Fiddler's Ferry
Inner
Hoyle
Thoresby
Dowsing
Ffestiniog
Connah's Quay
West Burton
Scroby
Sands
Ratcliffe-on-Soar
Carno
Rugeley
Sizewell
Rheidol
Penrhyddlan
Daw Mill
Gunfleet
Llidiart-y-waun
Sands
Tilbury
Kentish Flats
Didcot
Barking
Seabank
Kingsnorth
Aberthaw
Dungeness
Hinkley
Point
Wytch
Farm

ford University Press

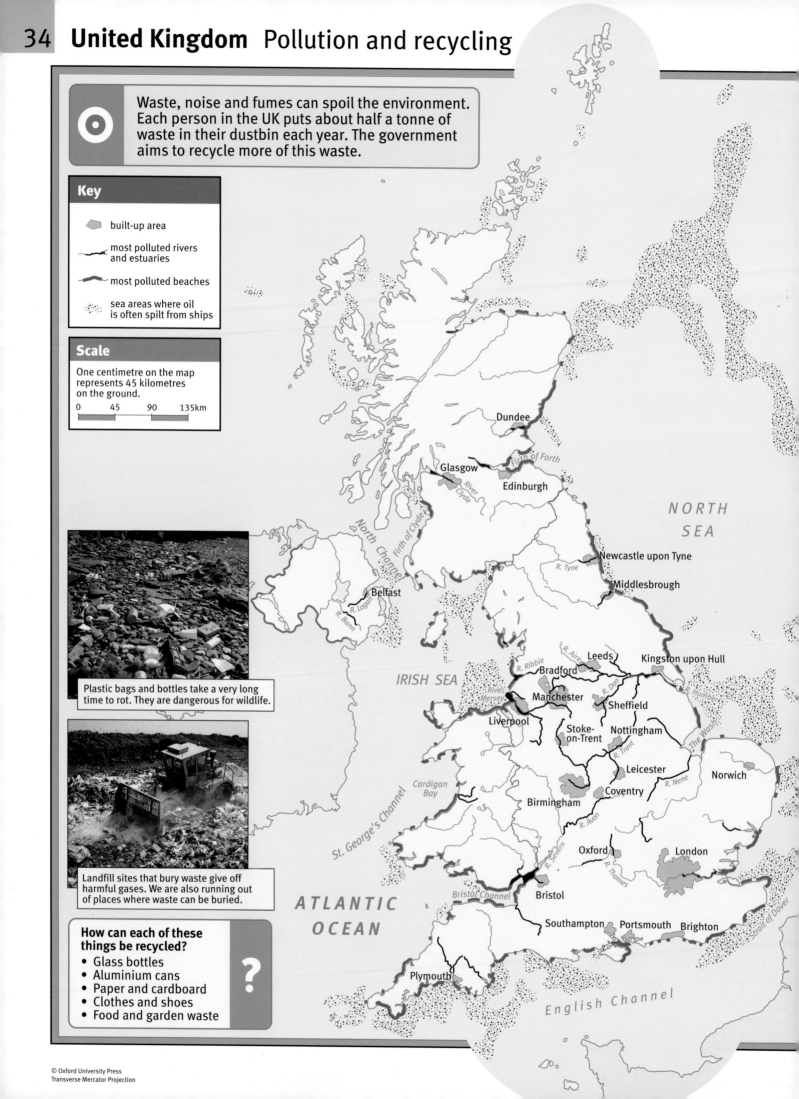

Waste, noise and fumes can spoil the environment. Each person in the UK puts about half a tonne of waste in their dustbin each year. The government aims to recycle more of this waste.

Key

- built-up area
- most polluted rivers and estuaries
- most polluted beaches
- sea areas where oil is often spilt from ships

Scale

One centimetre on the map represents 45 kilometres on the ground.

0   45   90   135km

Plastic bags and bottles take a very long time to rot. They are dangerous for wildlife.

Landfill sites that bury waste give off harmful gases. We are also running out of places where waste can be buried.

How can each of these things be recycled?

- Glass bottles
- Aluminium cans
- Paper and cardboard
- Clothes and shoes
- Food and garden waste

?

Dundee
Firth of Forth
Glasgow
River Clyde
Edinburgh

North Channel
Firth of Clyde

Belfast
R. Lagan
R. Bann

NORTH SEA

Newcastle upon Tyne
R. Tyne
Middlesbrough

IRISH SEA

R. Ribble
R. Aire
Leeds
Bradford
Kingston upon Hull
River Mersey
Manchester
R. Don
Sheffield
R. Humber
Liverpool
Stoke-on-Trent
Nottingham
The Wash
R. Trent
Leicester
R. Nene
Norwich
Cardigan Bay
Coventry
Birmingham
R. Avon
St. George's Channel
R. Severn
Oxford
London
R. Thames
Bristol Channel
Bristol

ATLANTIC OCEAN

Southampton
Portsmouth
Brighton
Strait of Dover

Plymouth

English Channel

Some parts of the country are specially protected because they are especially beautiful or have rare plants and animals. Some places that were important in history are also protected.

Key

- National Parks
- areas of outstanding scenery and beauty
- protected coast
- ✳ World Heritage site
- built-up area

Scale

One centimetre on the map represents 45 kilometres on the ground.

| 0 | 45 | 90 | 135km |

Which National Park is nearest to where you live? **?**

Protected coast
Pembrokeshire coast

World Heritage site
Ironbridge

National Park
Snowdonia

Area of outstanding scenery and beauty
The Cotswolds

Shetland

Hoy and West Mainland
✳ The Heart of Neolithic Orkney

Kyle of Tongue

South Lewis, Harris, and North Uist

Assynt Coigach

✳ St. Kilda

Wester Ross

The Cuillin Hills

Knoydart

Aberdeen

Cairngorms

Ben Nevis and Glen Coe

Loch na Keal, Isle of Mull

Loch Rannoch and Glen Lyon

Loch Lomond and the Trossachs

Knapdale

Jura

Old and New Towns of Edinburgh

Antonine Wall Edinburgh

Glasgow

North Arran

New Lanark

Upper Tweeddale

Giant's Causeway ✳

Antrim Coast and Glens

Sperrin

Belfast

Strangford Lough

Mourne

Northumberland

Hadrian's Wall ✳ Newcastle upon Tyne

North Pennines

✳ **Durham Cathedral/Castle**

Lake District

Yorkshire Dales Nidderdale

✳ **Fountain's Abbey/Studley Royal Park**

Forest of Bowland

North York Moors

Leeds

Saltaire ✳

Liverpool- Maritime Mercantile City ✳

Manchester

Anglesey

Clwydian Range

Liverpool

Sheffield

Lincolnshire Wolds

Castles/Town Walls of King Edward ✳

Peak District

Derwent Valley Mills ✳

Norfolk Coast

Pontcysyllte Aqueduct and Canal ✳

Stoke-on-Trent

Nottingham

Snowdonia

Ironbridge Gorge ✳

Lleyn

Shropshire Hills

Coventry

The Broads

Birmingham

Suffolk Coast and Heaths

Pembrokeshire Coast

Brecon Beacons

Wye Valley

Cotswolds ✳

Blenheim Palace

Chilterns

London

Blaenavon ✳

Oxford

Kew Gardens ✳

Tower of London ✳
✳ **Maritime Greenwich**

Gower

Cardiff

Bristol

North Wessex Downs

Bath

Westminster Palace/Abbey ✳

Canterbury Cathedral

Kent Downs

✳ **Stonehenge/Avebury**

South Downs

High Weald

Exmoor

Cranborne Chase

Blackdown Hills

Dorset

Isle of Wight

Dartmoor

Dorset and East Devon Coast

New Forest

Cornwall and West Devon Mining Landscape

Cornwall

Tamar Valley

Isles of Scilly

Roads and railways connect places within the UK. Ports, airports and the Channel Tunnel link the UK to the rest of Europe and beyond.

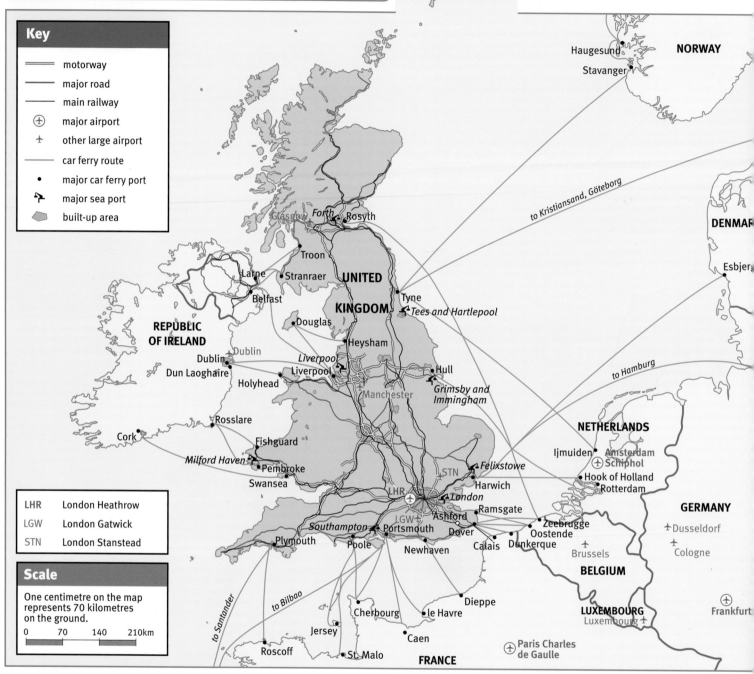

Key

═══	motorway
───	major road
───	main railway
✈ (circled)	major airport
✈	other large airport
───	car ferry route
•	major car ferry port
⚓	major sea port
▨	built-up area

LHR	London Heathrow
LGW	London Gatwick
STN	London Stanstead

Scale

One centimetre on the map represents 70 kilometres on the ground.

0   70   140   210km

Major car ferry port, Dover.

Major airport, London Heathrow.

Channel Tunnel terminal, Ashford.

If you were going to travel to France, which way would you go?

Holidays are time off work or school. **Tourism** is travelling to other places for a holiday.

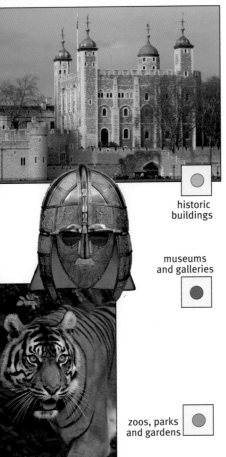

historic buildings

museums and galleries

zoos, parks and gardens

theme parks and piers

Top UK tourist attractions

Key

Symbol **colour** shows the type of tourist attraction

- ● historic buildings
- ● museums and galleries
- ● zoos, parks and gardens
- ● theme parks and piers

Symbol **size** shows how many people visit each year

- ○ over 2 million visitors
- ○ 1–2 million visitors
- ○ under 1 million visitors
- ▶ built-up area

Which of these tourist attractions would you most like to visit? **?**

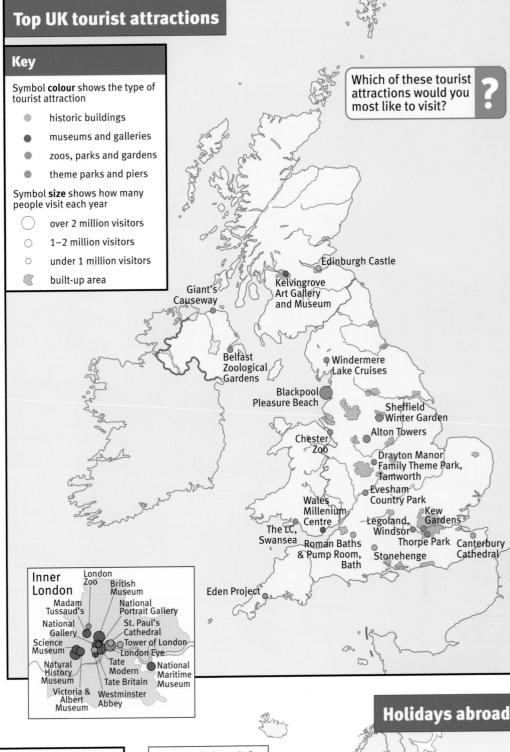

Edinburgh Castle

Giant's Causeway

Kelvingrove Art Gallery and Museum

Belfast Zoological Gardens

Windermere Lake Cruises

Blackpool Pleasure Beach

Sheffield Winter Garden

Chester Zoo

Alton Towers

Drayton Manor Family Theme Park, Tamworth

Evesham Country Park

Wales Millenium Centre

Legoland, Windsor

Kew Gardens

The LC, Swansea

Roman Baths & Pump Room, Bath

Thorpe Park

Stonehenge

Canterbury Cathedral

Eden Project

Inner London

London Zoo

British Museum

Madam Tussaud's

National Portrait Gallery

National Gallery

St. Paul's Cathedral

Science Museum

Tower of London

London Eye

Natural History Museum

Tate Modern

National Maritime Museum

Victoria & Albert Museum

Tate Britain

Westminster Abbey

Holidays in the UK and abroad

Number of holidays taken by people who live in the UK

- holidays in the UK
- holidays abroad

How is the pattern of where people go on holiday changing? **?**

millions

40
35
30
25
20
15
10
5
0

1971 1981 1991 2001

Holidays abroad

each symbol stands for 1 million British tourists

Canada

USA

Which countries are most popular? **?**

Europe is a continent of peninsulas and islands. The Ural Mountains form its eastern boundary.

Key

land height in metres above sea level

more than 2000m

1000 – 2000m

500 – 1000m

200 – 500m

less than 200 metres

land below sea level

▲ highest peaks with heights in metres

⌢ lake

~ river

Fact box

	area:	10 214 392km²
▲	**highest point:**	Mt. Elbrus 5 642m
▼	**lowest point:**	Caspian Sea 28m below sea level
	longest river:	River Volga 3 688km

Scale

One centimetre on the map represents 240 kilometres on the ground.

0   240   480   720km

Can you name the water that separates Great Britain from France? **?**

A B C D E F

3

20°W

Prime Meridian

0°

20°E

40°E

60°E

Europeans have settled all over the world and European languages can be heard in every other continent.

Arctic Circle

60°N

ICELAND
Reykjavik

N

ATLANTIC OCEAN

60°N

NORWAY

SWEDEN

FINLAND

RUSSIAN FEDERATION (RUSSIA)

NORTH SEA

BALTIC SEA

Oslo

Stockholm
Göteborg

Helsinki
Tallinn
ESTONIA

St. Petersburg

Nizhniy-Novgorod

Belfast
Edinburgh

REPUBLIC OF IRELAND
Dublin

UNITED KINGDOM
Manchester
Birmingham

Copenhagen
DENMARK

LATVIA
Riga

Moscow

LITHUANIA

KALININGRAD (Russia)

Vilnius

Minsk
BELARUS

NETHERLANDS
Hamburg

London
Rotterdam
Amsterdam

BELGIUM
Brussels
Düsseldorf

GERMANY
Berlin

POLAND

Warsaw

2

Kiev
Kharkov

Volgograd

Paris

LUXEMBOURG
Luxembourg

Prague
CZECH REP.

Krakow

UKRAINE

Donets'k
Rostov-on-Don

FRANCE

Bordeaux

Bern
Munich

Lyons

SWITZERLAND
LIECHTENSTEIN

Vienna
AUSTRIA

SLOVAKIA
Bratislava

Budapest

MOLDOVA
Chisinau
Odessa

40°N

Oporto

Ljubljana
Milan

SLOVENIA
Zagreb
CROATIA

HUNGARY

ROMANIA
Bucharest

BLACK SEA

GEORGIA
T'bilisi

PORTUGAL

SPAIN

ANDORRA
Marseilles

Lyons

ITALY

SAN MARINO

BOSNIA-HERZEGOVINA
Sarajevo

Belgrade

SERBIA
Pristina

Sofia
BULGARIA

Lisbon
Madrid

Barcelona
Valencia

MONACO

Rome

Naples

Podgorica
MONTENEGRO

KOSOVO
Skopje
FYRO MACEDONIA

Istanbul

Ankara
TURKEY

Gibraltar (UK)

Seville

Ceuta (Sp.)
Melilla (Sp.)

MEDITERRANEAN

Tiranë
ALBANIA

GREECE

Izmir

Adana

MOROCCO

ALGERIA

TUNISIA

SEA

Valletta
MALTA

Athens

Nicosia
CYPRUS

SYRIA

IRAQ

LEBANON
ISRAEL

1

LIBYA

EGYPT

JORDAN

SAUDI ARABIA

Tropic of Cancer

20°E

40°E

Key

colours show countries

ITALY country names are labelled like this

capital cities

other important cities

Fact box

population:	655 884 785 people *	
largest country:	Ukraine 603 698km²	
country with most people:	Germany 82 698 000	
largest city:	Istanbul, Turkey 9 946 000	

* does not include Russian Federation

Many languages are spoken in Europe How many can you name?

B C D

© Oxford University Press

Low, flat land and shallow seas stretch all the way from the UK to Moscow and beyond.

Norway's fiords are long narrow fingers of sea between steep mountains.

ICELAND

Ísafjördur
Reykjavik
Akureyri
Mount Hekla 1491
Höfn

Arctic Circle

NORWEGIAN SEA

Vesteralen Is.
Lofoten Is.
Bodo

ATLANTIC OCEAN

Faroe Islands (Den.)

Shetland Islands

Outer Hebrides
Orkney Islands

N O R W A Y

Scandinavia

Trondheim

Galdhøpiggen 2470m

Bergen
Stavanger

S W E D E N

Oslo
Uppsa
Lake Vänern
Stockhol

1344m
Ben Nevis
Inverness
Aberdeen
Glasgow
Dundee
Edinburgh
Newcastle upon Tyne

Galway
Belfast

REPUBLIC OF IRELAND
Dublin

Manchester
Liverpool
Leeds

UNITED KINGDOM

Cork

Birmingham

Cardiff
Bristol

Plymouth
Land's End
Isles of Scilly

Norwich
London
The Hague
Rotterdam
Southampton
Strait of Dover
English Channel

NORTH SEA

Skagerrak

DENMARK
Ålborg
Århus
Copenhagen
Odense
Bornholm
Malmö

Kattegat
Lake Vättern
Göteborg
Jönköping

Kiel
Rostock

Frisian Is.
Hamburg
Bremen R. Elbe
Szczecin

NETHERLANDS
Amsterdam
Hannover
Berlin
Pozna

Channel Islands
Brest
le Havre
Rouen
Reims

Calais
Lille
Antwerp
BELGIUM
Brussels
Essen
Düsseldorf
Cologne
Bonn
LUXEMBOURG
Luxembourg

GERMANY
Leipzig
Dresden
Wrocla

R. Oder

Frankfurt-am-Main
Prague

CZECH RE
Brno

Rennes
le Mans
Paris
Nancy
Nantes
Tours
Orléans
Dijon
Basel
FRANCE

River Loire
River Seine
River Saône
River Rhine
Strasbourg
Stuttgart
Nuremberg

River Danube

Munich
Salzburg
Innsbruck
Bern
SWITZERLAND
Zürich
LIECHTENSTEIN

Linz
Bratisla
Vienna
AUSTRIA

Bay of Biscay

30°W   20°W   10°W   70°N   Prime Meridian   0°   10°E
60°N
50°N
10°W

© Oxford University Press
Conical Orthomorphic Projection

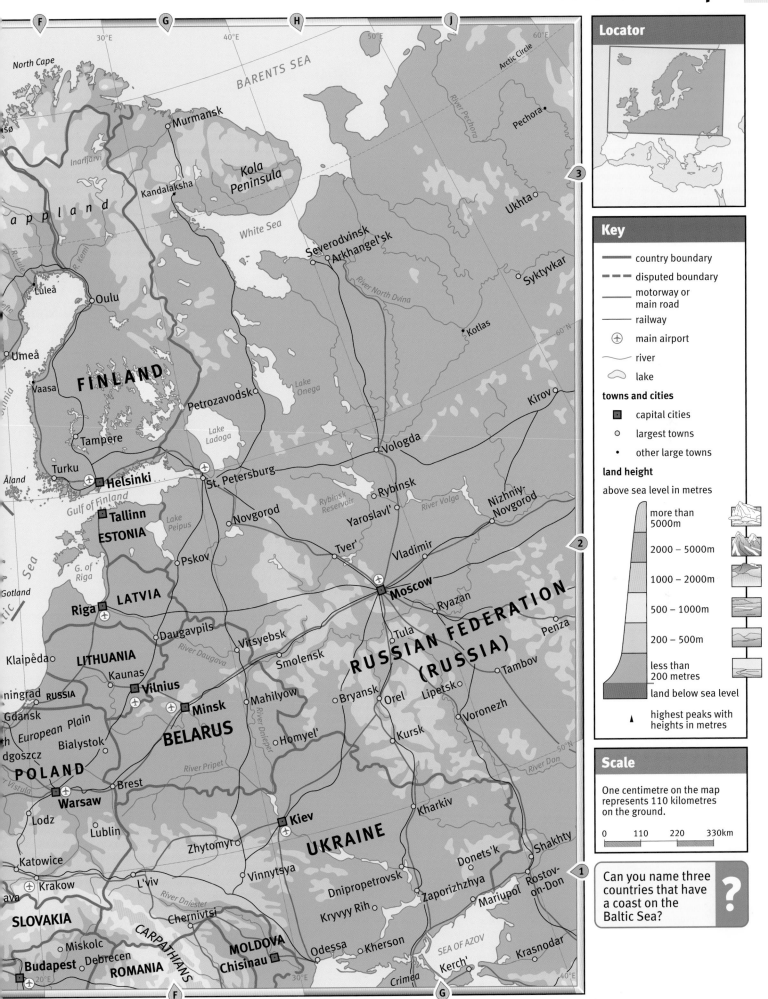

Locator

Key

———	country boundary
– – –	disputed boundary
———	motorway or main road
———	railway
⊕	main airport
⌒	river
⬭	lake

towns and cities

▣	capital cities
○	largest towns
•	other large towns

land height
above sea level in metres

| more than 5000m |
| 2000 – 5000m |
| 1000 – 2000m |
| 500 – 1000m |
| 200 – 500m |
| less than 200 metres |
| land below sea level |

▲ highest peaks with heights in metres

Scale

One centimetre on the map represents 110 kilometres on the ground.

0   110   220   330km

Can you name three countries that have a coast on the Baltic Sea?

North Cape

BARENTS SEA

Murmansk

Inarijärvi

Kandalaksha

Kola Peninsula

White Sea

Severodvinsk
Arkhangel'sk

River North Dvina

Pechora

Ukhta

Syktyvkar

Kotlas

Luleå

Oulu

R. Kemi

Umeå

Vaasa

FINLAND

Petrozavodsk

Lake Onega

Kirov

Tampere

Lake Ladoga

Turku

Helsinki

Åland

St. Petersburg

Vologda

Rybinsk

Nizhniy-Novgorod

Gulf of Finland

Lake Peipus

Novgorod

Rybinsk Reservoir

River Volga

Yaroslavl'

Tallinn

ESTONIA

Pskov

Tver'

Vladimir

Gotland

G. of Riga

Riga

LATVIA

Moscow

Ryazan

RUSSIAN FEDERATION
(RUSSIA)

Daugavpils

Vitsyebsk

Tula

Penza

River Daugava

Klaipėda

LITHUANIA

Smolensk

ningrad RUSSIA

Kaunas

Vilnius

Mahilyow

Bryansk

Orel

Lipetsk

Tambov

Gdansk

Minsk

River Dnieper

Voronezh

European Plain

Bialystok

BELARUS

Homyel'

Kursk

dgoszcz

POLAND

River Pripet

River Don

Brest

Kharkiv

Warsaw

Lodz

Kiev

Lublin

Zhytomyr

UKRAINE

Donets'k

Shakhty

Katowice

Vinnytsya

Dnipropetrovsk

Zaporizhzhya

Rostov-on-Don

Krakow

L'viv

River Dniester

Kryvyy Rih

Mariupol

va

Chernivtsi

SLOVAKIA

CARPATHIANS

Odessa

Kherson

SEA OF AZOV

Krasnodar

Miskolc

Debrecen

MOLDOVA

Budapest

ROMANIA

Chisinau

Kerch'

Crimea

Arctic Circle

60°N

50°N

20°E   30°E   40°E   50°E   60°E

The countries of southern Europe share a coastline on the Mediterranean Sea.

UNITED KINGDOM
Norwich
Cardiff
Bristol
London
Plymouth
Southampton
NETHERLANDS
The Hague
Rotterdam
Amsterdam
Essen
Antwerp
BELGIUM
Brussels
Bonn
Lille
Calais
Kiel
Hamburg
Rostock
Bremen
R. Elbe
Berlin
Hannover
Düsseldorf
Cologne
GERMANY
Leipzig
Dresden
Szczecin
R. Oder
Poz
Wrocla
Land's End
Isles of Scilly
English Channel
Strait of Dover
Channel Islands
le Havre
Rouen
Reims
LUXEMBOURG
Luxembourg
Frankfurt-am-Main
Nancy
Strasbourg
Stuttgart
Nuremberg
Prague
CZECH R
Brest
Rennes
le Mans
Paris
Orléans
Dijon
Basel
Munich
Salzburg
Linz
Bratis
Vienna
Bay of Biscay
Nantes
Tours
FRANCE
Limoges
Clermont-Ferrand
R. Saône
River Loire
Lyons
Geneva
4807m
Mont Blanc
Bern
SWITZERLAND
Zürich
Lake Geneva
LIECHTENSTEIN
Innsbruck
AUSTRIA
Graz
A Coruña
Cape Finisterre
Gijón
Oviedo
Santander
Bilbao
Bordeaux
St-Étienne
MASSIF CENTRAL
Grenoble
Milan
Venice
Trieste
Ljubljana
SLOVENIA
Zag
Vigo
Cantabrian Mts.
León
San Sebastián
Toulouse
PYRÉNÉES
Nîmes
Avignon
Turin
Verona
Módena
Bologna
River Po
CROATIA
Oporto
River Douro
Valladolid
Zaragoza
ANDORRA
Marseilles
Nice
MONACO
Genoa
Florence
SAN MARINO
Split
ADRIATIC
PORTUGAL
River Duero
SPAIN
Madrid
Barcelona
Corsica (France)
Elba
ITALY
APPENNINES
Coimbra
Lisbon
River Tagus
River Guadiana
Valencia
Balearic Islands
Ajaccio
Rome
Sierra Morena
River Guadalquivir
Murcia
Alicante
Palma
Menorca
Mallorca
Ibiza
Sardinia (Italy)
Sassari
TYRRHENIAN SEA
Naples
Vesuvius 1277m
Salerno
Bar
Faro
Seville
Jerez de la Frontera
Cartagena
Cape St. Vincent
Cádiz
Sierra Nevada
Málaga
Gibraltar (UK)
Ceuta (Sp.)
Tétouan
Cagliari
Palermo
Messina
Mt Etna 3323m
Sicily
Catania
Regg
Calab
Tara
Tangier
Oran
Melilla (Sp.)
Algiers
Blida
Bejaïa
Skikda
Annaba
Bizerte
Tunis
MALTA
Valletta
Meknès
Fès
Oudja
Sidi-Bel-Abbès
Ech Cheliff
Constantine
Sétif
Sousse
Bou Saâda
Djelfa
Biskra
Tébessa
TUNISIA
Gafsa
Sfax
Gabès
MOROCCO
ATLAS MOUNTAINS
Bouârfa
Aïn Sefra
El Bayadh
Touggourt
Tozeur
Béchar
Prime Meridian
0°
El Golea
30°N
ALGERIA
Hassi Messaoud
Tripoli
Misratah
LIBYA

Hot, dry summers make the Mediterranean coast a popular choice for holidays.

MEDITERRANEAN SEA

Key

⎯⎯⎯	country boundary
- - - -	disputed boundary
⎯⎯⎯	motorway or main road
⎯⎯⎯	railway
⊕	main airport
⎯⎯⎯	river
◠	lake

towns and cities

▣	capital cities
○	largest towns
•	other large towns

land height

above sea level in metres

more than 5000m	
2000 – 5000m	
1000 – 2000m	
500 – 1000m	
200 – 500m	
less than 200 metres	
land below sea level	
▲	highest peaks with heights in metres

Scale

One centimetre on the map represents 110 kilometres on the ground.

0   110   220   330km

Can you name six islands in the Mediterranean Sea? **?**

© Oxford University Press

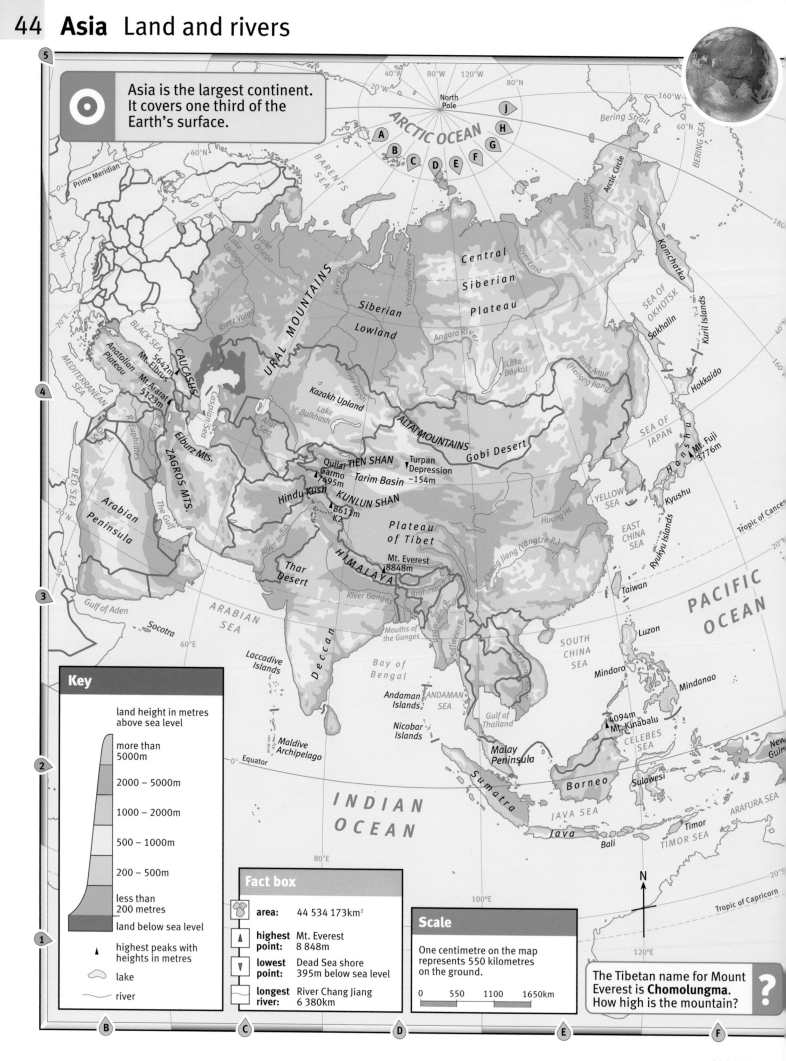

Asia is the largest continent. It covers one third of the Earth's surface.

Key

land height in metres above sea level

more than 5000m

2000 – 5000m

1000 – 2000m

500 – 1000m

200 – 500m

less than 200 metres

land below sea level

▲ highest peaks with heights in metres

lake

river

Fact box

	area:	44 534 173km²
▲	**highest point:**	Mt. Everest 8 848m
▼	**lowest point:**	Dead Sea shore 395m below sea level
	longest river:	River Chang Jiang 6 380km

Scale

One centimetre on the map represents 550 kilometres on the ground.

0   550   1100   1650km

The Tibetan name for Mount Everest is **Chomolungma**. How high is the mountain?

?

ARCTIC OCEAN

North Pole

Prime Meridian

BARENTS SEA

URAL MOUNTAINS

Lake Ladoga

Lake Onega

River Ob

Yenisey River

Central Siberian Plateau

River Lena

Siberian Lowland

Angara River

Lake Baykal

River Amur (Heilong Jiang)

Kamchatka

SEA OF OKHOTSK

Bering Strait

BERING SEA

Arctic Circle

R. Kolyma

Kuril Islands

Sakhalin

Hokkaido

SEA OF JAPAN

Honshu

Mt. Fuji 3776m

Kyushu

Ryukyu Islands

EAST CHINA SEA

YELLOW SEA

Huang He

Chang Jiang (Yangtze R.)

Taiwan

PACIFIC OCEAN

MEDITERRANEAN SEA

BLACK SEA

Anatolian Plateau

Mt. Elbrus 5642m

CAUCASUS

Mt. Ararat 5123m

Caspian Sea

Elburz Mts.

ZAGROS MTS.

Aral Sea

Lake Balkhash

Kazakh Upland

River Irtysh

ALTAI MOUNTAINS

Gobi Desert

Turpan Depression -154m

TIEN SHAN

Qullai Garmo 7495m

Tarim Basin

KUNLUN SHAN

Plateau of Tibet

Dead Sea

R. Tigris

Euphrates

The Gulf

RED SEA

Arabian Peninsula

Hindu Kush

8611m K2

Mt. Everest 8848m

HIMALAYA

River Indus

Thar Desert

River Ganges

Brahmaputra

Gulf of Aden

Socotra

ARABIAN SEA

Deccan

Mouths of the Ganges

Bay of Bengal

Irrawaddy R.

Salween R.

Mekong R.

SOUTH CHINA SEA

Luzon

Mindoro

Mindanao

Laccadive Islands

Maldive Archipelago

Andaman Islands

ANDAMAN SEA

Nicobar Islands

Gulf of Thailand

Malay Peninsula

4094m Mt. Kinabalu

CELEBES SEA

Borneo

Sulawesi

New Guinea

Equator

INDIAN OCEAN

Sumatra

JAVA SEA

Java

Bali

Timor

TIMOR SEA

ARAFURA SEA

Tropic of Cancer

Tropic of Capricorn

N

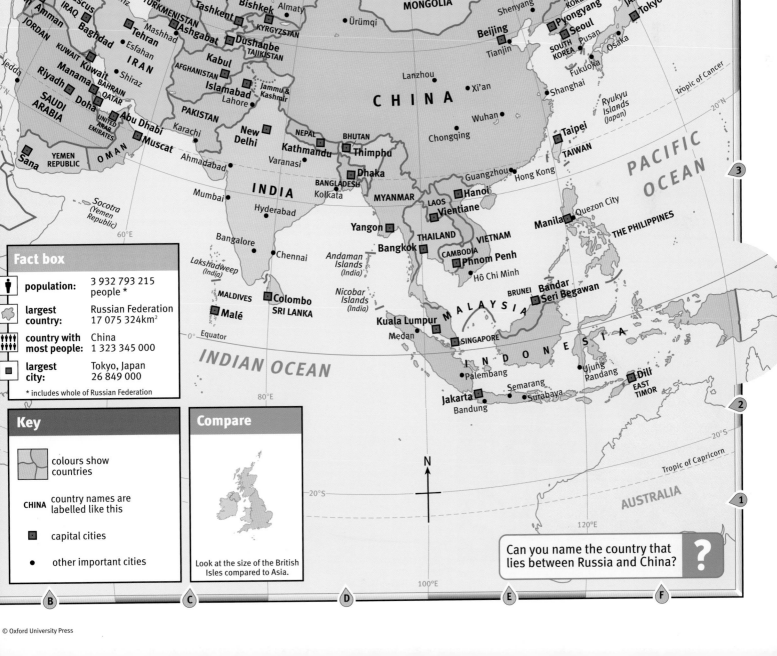

Of all the continents, Asia has the greatest variety of landscapes and cultures.

ARCTIC OCEAN

North Pole

A B C D E F G H J

St. Petersburg

Nizhniy-Novgorod

Moscow

Perm

RUSSIAN FEDERATION (RUSSIA)

Chelyabinsk

Volgograd

Omsk

Novosibirsk

Ankara
Istanbul

TURKEY
GEORGIA Tbilisi
Adana ARMENIA Yerevan
LEBANON SYRIA AZERBAIJAN
Beirut Aleppo Baku
ISRAEL Damascus Tabriz
Jerusalem IRAQ
Amman
JORDAN Baghdad

KAZAKHSTAN

Astana

Kuril Islands (Russia)

Sapporo

Harbin

UZBEKISTAN
Tashkent
Bishkek
Almaty
KYRGYZSTAN

Ulan Bator

MONGOLIA

Shenyang

NORTH KOREA
Pyongyang

JAPAN
Tokyo

Seoul

TURKMENISTAN
Ashgabat
Mashhad
Dushanbe
TAJIKISTAN

Tehran

KUWAIT
Kuwait
Esfahan
IRAN
Manama BAHRAIN
Riyadh Shiraz
QATAR
Doha
UNITED ARAB EMIRATES
Abu Dhabi

Kabul
AFGHANISTAN
Islamabad
Lahore
Jammu & Kashmir

Beijing

SOUTH KOREA
Pusan
Tianjin
Osaka
Fukuoka

Lanzhou

Xi'an

CHINA

Ryukyu Islands (Japan)

Tropic of Cancer

SAUDI ARABIA

Jedda

Muscat

OMAN

Sana
YEMEN REPUBLIC

PAKISTAN

Karachi

New Delhi

NEPAL
Kathmandu

BHUTAN
Thimphu

Ahmadabad

Varanasi

Wuhan

Chongqing

Dhaka

Taipei

TAIWAN

Socotra (Yemen Republic)

Mumbai

INDIA

BANGLADESH
Kolkata

Guangzhou

Hong Kong

PACIFIC OCEAN

Hyderabad

MYANMAR

LAOS
Hanoi

Bangalore

Yangon

Vientiane

Manila

Quezon City

Fact box

Chennai

THAILAND

VIETNAM

Andaman Islands (India)

Bangkok

CAMBODIA
Phnom Penh

THE PHILIPPINES

Lakshadweep (India)

Hô Chi Minh

	population:	3 932 793 215 people *
	largest country:	Russian Federation 17 075 324km²
	country with most people:	China 1 323 345 000
	largest city:	Tokyo, Japan 26 849 000

* includes whole of Russian Federation

MALDIVES
Malé

Colombo
SRI LANKA

Nicobar Islands (India)

BRUNEI Bandar Seri Begawan

M A L A Y S I A

Kuala Lumpur
Medan

SINGAPORE

I N D O N E S I A

Equator

INDIAN OCEAN

Palembang

Ujung Pandang

Dili
EAST TIMOR

Jakarta
Bandung

Semarang

Surabaya

Key

colours show countries

CHINA country names are labelled like this

capital cities

• other important cities

Compare

Look at the size of the British Isles compared to Asia.

N

Tropic of Capricorn

AUSTRALIA

Can you name the country that lies between Russia and China?

?

Call centres provide information or answer people's questions by telephone. This call centre is in Bangalore.

India is an important centre of the computer software industry. Several million people work at making computer programs.

PAMIRS
TAJIKISTAN
Khorog

7690m
Gilgit
▲K2 (Qogir Feng, Godwin Austen) 8611m
Rutog

shawar
Srinagar
JAMMU AND KASHMIR
Leh

Islamabad
Rawalpindi
Jammu
R. Indus
R. Jhelum

Gujranwala
Lahore
Amritsar
Faisalabad
Chandigarh

Multan
a Ghazi Khan
Ludhiana
Dehra Dun
River Sutlej

Bahawalpur
Desert
Meerut

Bikaner
New Delhi
Delhi
R. Yamuna
Bareilly

myar an
Jaipur
Agra
R. Ghaghara
Lucknow
Gorakhpur

Jodhpur
River Ganges
Kanpur
R. Gomati
Muzaffarpur

Kota
Gwalior
R. Chambal
R. Banas
Jhansi
Allahabad
Varanasi
Patna
Bhagalpur

Murwara
Dhanbad
Asanol

Ahmadabad
Bhopal
Jabalpur
R. Son
Jamshedpur
Kolkata
Khulna

Vadodara
Indore
R. Narmada
Bilaspur
Hirakud Reservoir
Kharagpur

nagar
Bharuch
R. Tapi
Raipur
Sambalpur

Surat
Burhanpur
Nagpur
R. Mahanadi
Cuttack

Dhule
Amravati

Nashik
Aurangabad
R. Godavari
Chandrapur

umbai
Pune
Nizamabad
R. Indravati
Brahmapur

Deccan
R. Godavari

Solapur
R. Bhima
Hyderabad
Vishakhapatnam

Kolhapur
Bijapur
R. Krishna
Rajahmundry

Raichur
Vijayawada

Belgaum
Bellary
R. Penner

Nellore

Mangalore
Bangalore
Vellore
Chennai

Mysore
EASTERN GHATS

WESTERN GHATS
Pondicherry

Calicut
Salem

Coimbatore
Tiruchchirappalli

Cochin
Jaffna
SRI LANKA

Quilon
Trincomalee

Trivandrum
Batticaloa

Nagercoil
Puttalam

Colombo
Kandy

Badulla
Galle

Laccadive Islands

Gulf of Khambhat

kot
Gandhi Sagar

CHINA

HIMALAYA
NEPAL

8091m
Annapurna
Mount Everest 8848m
Lhaze

Kathmandu
Darjiling

Thimphu
BHUTAN

Lhasa
Nyingchi

Yarlung Zangbo (Tsangpo R.)
Dibrugarh

Guwahati
Nagaon
Shillong

Brahmaputra R.
Imphal

BANGLADESH
Dhaka

Chittagong
Monywa
Mandalay

River Chindwin

MYANMAR (BURMA)

Arakan Yoma

Sittwe

Irrawaddy R.

Sandoway
Pye

Yangon

Bassein

Mouths of the Irrawaddy

Bay of Bengal

Andaman Islands

Port Blair

ANDAMAN SEA

INDIAN OCEAN

Mouths of the Ganges

Tropic of Cancer

Nu Jiang (Salween R.)
Lancang Jiang (Mekong R.)

80°E
90°E
30°N
20°N
10°N

Mumbai is sometimes called **Bollywood**. Can you find out what are made there?

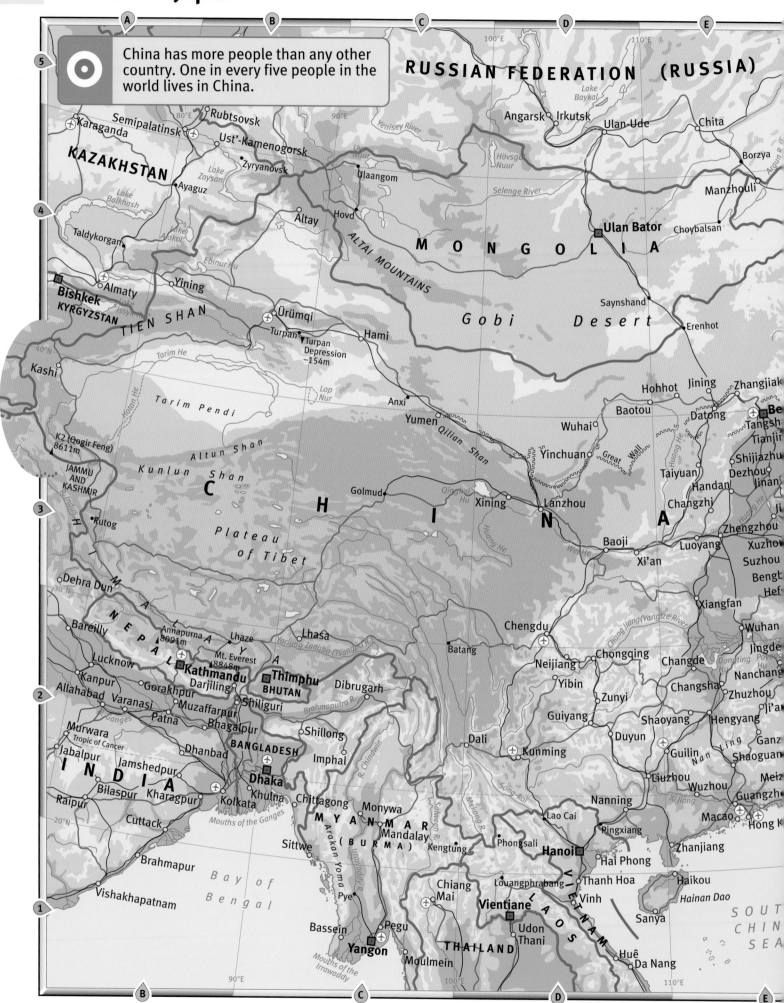

China has more people than any other country. One in every five people in the world lives in China.

RUSSIAN FEDERATION (RUSSIA)

KAZAKHSTAN

Karaganda
Semipalatinsk
Rubtsovsk
Ust'-Kamenogorsk
Zyryanovsk
Altay
Hovd
Ulaangom
Lake Zaysan
Ayaguz
Lake Balkhash
Taldykorgan
Lake Alakol'
Ebinur Hu
ALTAI MOUNTAINS
Lake Baykal
Angarsk
Irkutsk
Ulan-Ude
Chita
Borzya
Manzhouli
Selenge River
MONGOLIA
Ulan Bator
Choybalsan
Gobi Desert
Saynshand
Erenhot

Almaty
Bishkek
KYRGYZSTAN
Yining
Lake Issyk-kul
TIEN SHAN
Ürümqi
Turpan
Turpan Depression −154m
Hami
Hohhot
Jining
Zhangjiak
Baotou
Datong
Be
Tangsh
Tianjin
Shijiazhu
Dezhou
Jinan

Kashi
Tarim He
Hotan He
Tarim Pendi
Lop Nur
Anxi
Yumen
Qilian Shan
Wuhai
Yinchuan
Great Wall
Taiyuan
Handan

K2 (Qogir Feng) 8611m
JAMMU AND KASHMIR
Altun Shan
Kunlun Shan
Golmud
Qinghai Hu
Xining
Lanzhou
Changzhi
Zhengzhou

Rutog
C
H
Plateau of Tibet
I
N
Baoji
Wei He
Xi'an
Luoyang
Xuzho
Suzhou
Bengb
Hef
Ji

Dehra Dun
Bareilly
Lucknow
Kanpur
Allahabad
Varanasi
Annapurna 8091m
Lhaze
Mt. Everest 8848m
Kathmandu
NEPAL
Darjiling
Gorakhpur
Thimphu
BHUTAN
Lhasa
Yarlung Zangbo (Tsangpo R.)
Dibrugarh
Brahmaputra R.
Chengdu
Batang
Neijiang
Chongqing
Changde
Xiangfan
Wuhan
Jingde
Nanchang
Dongting Hu
Changsha
Zhuzhou
Ji'a

Murwara
Jabalpur
Jamshedpur
INDIA
Bilaspur
Muzaffarpur
Patna
Bhagalpur
Dhanbad
BANGLADESH
Shiliguri
Shillong
Imphal
Dhaka
Dali
Kunming
Yibin
Guiyang
Duyun
Zunyi
Shaoyang
Hengyang
Guilin
Shaoguan
Nan Ying
Ganz

Raipur
Kharagpur
Kolkata
Khulna
Chittagong
Monywa
Mouths of the Ganges
MYANMAR
Mandalay
(BURMA)
Kengtung
Phongsali
Lao Cai
Nanning
Pingxiang
Liuzhou
Wuzhou
Zhanjiang
Guangzh
Macao
Hong K
Meiz

Cuttack
Tropic of Cancer
Brahmapur
Arakan Yoma
Sittwe
Pye
Irrawaddy R.
Salween R.
Mekong R.
Chiang Mai
Louangphrabang
Hanoi
Hai Phong
Haikou
Hainan Dao
Thanh Hoa
Vinh
LAOS
VIETNAM
Sanya

Vishakhapatnam
Bay of Bengal
Bassein
Pegu
Yangon
Moulmein
Mouths of the Irrawaddy
THAILAND
Udon Thani
Vientiane
Huê
Da Nang
SOUT
CHIN
SEA

© Oxford University Press
Conical Orthomorphic Projection

Map Labels

Syan Ling
River Amur
Blagoveshchensk
Komsomol'sk-na-Amure
Sakhalin
SEA OF OKHOTSK
Khabarovsk
Nenjiang
Bei'an
Hegang
Jiamusi
Qiqihar
Shuangyashan
Daqing
Harbin
Jixi
aicheng
Mudanjiang
Yuzhno-Sakhalinsk
Wakkanai
Changchun
Jilin
Vladivostok
Asahikawa
Kushiro
Siping
Otaru
Hokkaido
Sapporo
Shenyang
Fushun
Tonghua
Chongjin
Hakodate
Anshan
Kimchaek
Aomori
Hachinohe
NORTH KOREA
Morioka
nuangdao
Dandong
Hamhung
Akita
SEA OF JAPAN
Pyongyang
Kangnung
Niigata
Sendai
Korea Bay
Dalian
Kangnung
SOUTH KOREA
Seoul
Tokyo
Yantai
Inchon
Pohang
Yokohama
Kawasaki
Taejon
Tottori
Kyoto
Nagoya
3776m Mt. Fuji
Qingdao
Taegu
Kobe
Osaka
YELLOW SEA
Pusan
Hiroshima
Kochi
Kwangju
Kita-Kyushu
Shikoku
Lianyungang
Fukuoka
Qingjiang
Cheju do
Nagasaki
Kyushu
Miyazaki
jing
Changzhou
EAST CHINA SEA
Kagoshima
u
Shanghai
Wuxi
gzhou
Ningbo
PACIFIC OCEAN
Ryukyu Islands
Wenzhou
Okinawa
anping
Tropic of Cancer
Fuzhou
Taipei
amen
Taichung
TAIWAN
Tainan
Kaohsiung
Luzon Strait
Laoag
Luzon
THE PHILIPPINES
Dagupan
Manila
Quezon City

More and more of the things people use are made in Chinese factories.

Key

——	country boundary
– – –	disputed boundary
——	motorway or main road
——	railway
⊕	main airport
~	river
⌒	lake

towns and cities

■ capital cities
○ largest towns
• other large towns

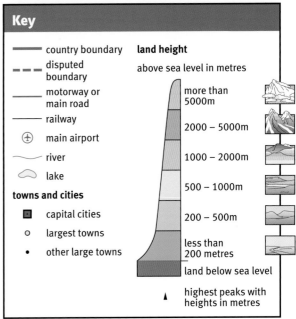

land height

above sea level in metres

more than 5000m
2000 – 5000m
1000 – 2000m
500 – 1000m
200 – 500m
less than 200 metres
land below sea level

▲ highest peaks with heights in metres

Scale

One centimetre on the map represents 180 kilometres on the ground.

0   180   360   540km

Locator

Japan is a country of islands. Can you name the largest island? **?**

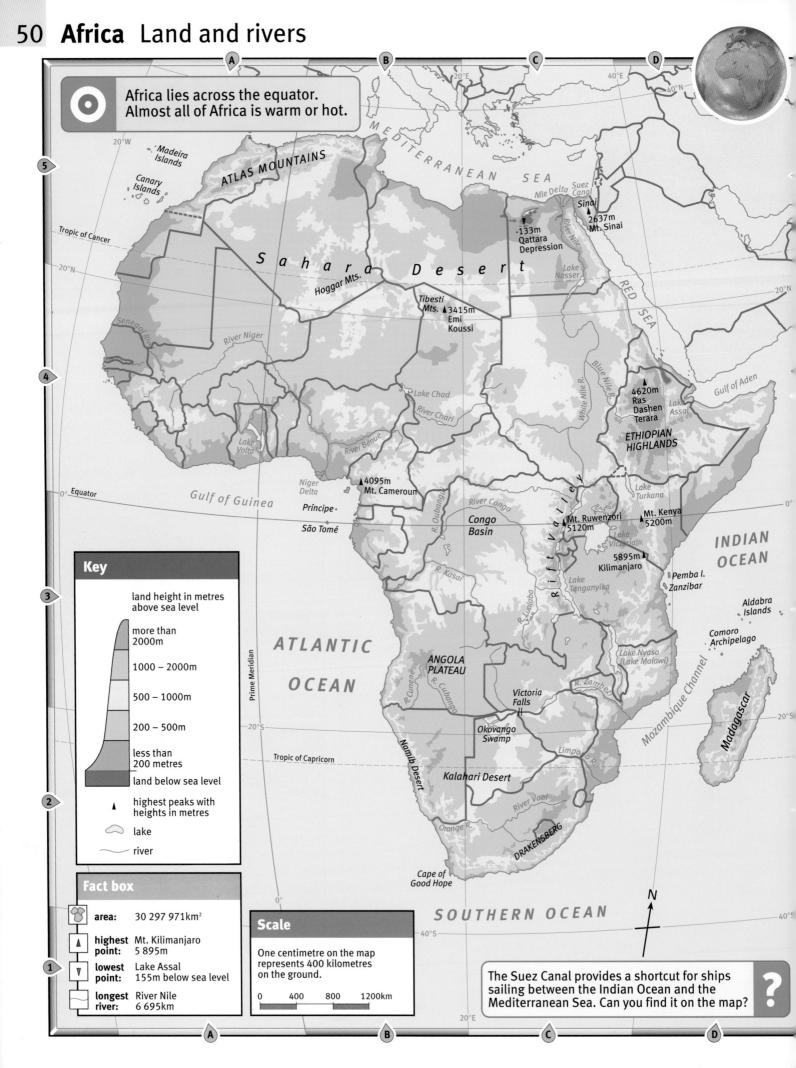

Africa lies across the equator. Almost all of Africa is warm or hot.

A · B · C · D

MEDITERRANEAN SEA

Madeira Islands
Canary Islands
ATLAS MOUNTAINS

Tropic of Cancer
20°N

S a h a r a   D e s e r t

Hoggar Mts.

Nile Delta
Suez Canal
Sinai
-133m Qattara Depression
2637m Mt. Sinai

RED SEA

Tibesti Mts. ▲3415m Emi Koussi

Lake Nasser

Senegal R.

River Niger

Lake Chad

River Chari

White Nile R.
Blue Nile R.

4620m Ras Dashen Terara
Lake Assal

Gulf of Aden

ETHIOPIAN HIGHLANDS

River Benue

Lake Volta

Niger Delta
▲4095m Mt. Cameroun

Príncipe
São Tomé

Gulf of Guinea

Equator 0°

River Oubangui

River Congo

Congo Basin

Mt. Ruwenzori ▲5120m

Lake Turkana

Mt. Kenya ▲5200m

INDIAN OCEAN

R. Kasai

Lake Victoria

5895m ▲ Kilimanjaro

Pemba I.
Zanzibar

Aldabra Islands

R. Lualaba

Rift Valley

Lake Tanganyika

Comoro Archipelago

Key

land height in metres above sea level

more than 2000m

1000 – 2000m

500 – 1000m

200 – 500m

less than 200 metres

land below sea level

▲ highest peaks with heights in metres

lake

river

ATLANTIC OCEAN

Prime Meridian

ANGOLA PLATEAU

R. Cunene
R. Cubango

Lake Nyasa (Lake Malawi)

Mozambique Channel

Madagascar

20°S

Victoria Falls

R. Zambezi

Tropic of Capricorn

Okovango Swamp

Namib Desert

Kalahari Desert

Limpopo R.

River Vaal

Orange R.

DRAKENSBERG

Cape of Good Hope

Fact box

🗺	**area:**	30 297 971km²
▲	**highest point:**	Mt. Kilimanjaro 5 895m
▼	**lowest point:**	Lake Assal 155m below sea level
	longest river:	River Nile 6 695km

Scale

One centimetre on the map represents 400 kilometres on the ground.

0   400   800   1200km

SOUTHERN OCEAN

N

The Suez Canal provides a shortcut for ships sailing between the Indian Ocean and the Mediterranean Sea. Can you find it on the map?

?

Many people in Africa live in villages but there are also very big cities.

SPAIN

Madeira (Portugal)

Tropic of Cancer

Canary Islands (Spain)

MOROCCO
Rabat
Casablanca
Marrakech

Algiers

Tunis
TUNISIA

Tripoli

MEDITERRANEAN SEA

Benghazi
Alexandria
Cairo
El Giza

IRAQ

IRAN

Laâyoune
WESTERN SAHARA

ALGERIA

LIBYA

EGYPT

RED SEA

SAUDI ARABIA

MAURITANIA
Nouakchott

MALI

NIGER

CHAD

Khartoum

SUDAN

ERITREA
Asmara

YEMEN REPUBLIC

Dakar
SENEGAL
Banjul
THE GAMBIA
Bissau
GUINEA-BISSAU
GUINEA
Conakry
Freetown
SIERRA LEONE
Monrovia
LIBERIA

Bamako

Niamey

BURKINA
Ouagadougou

BENIN
TOGO
GHANA
Yamoussoukro
Accra
Abidjan
CÔTE D'IVOIRE
Lomé

NIGERIA
Abuja

Ndjamena

Lagos

CAMEROON
Malabo
Yaoundé

CENTRAL AFRICAN REPUBLIC
Bangui

Ndjamena

Djibouti
DJIBOUTI
Addis Ababa

ETHIOPIA

SOMALIA
Mogadishu

Equator

EQUATORIAL GUINEA
São Tomé
Libreville
SÃO TOMÉ AND PRÍNCIPE

GABON
CONGO

DEMOCRATIC REPUBLIC OF CONGO

UGANDA
Kampala

Kigali
RWANDA
Bujumbura
BURUNDI

KENYA
Nairobi

Mombasa

INDIAN OCEAN

Brazzaville
Kinshasa

CABINDA (Angola)

TANZANIA
Dodoma
Dar es Salaam

Aldabra Is. (Seychelles)

Ascension I. (UK)

Luanda

ATLANTIC OCEAN

Prime Meridian

St. Helena (UK)

ANGOLA

ZAMBIA
Lusaka

MALAWI
Lilongwe

Moroni
COMOROS

MADAGASCAR

Harare
ZIMBABWE
Beira

Antananarivo

MOZAMBIQUE

Tropic of Capricorn

NAMIBIA
Windhoek
Walvis Bay

BOTSWANA

Gaborone
Pretoria
Maputo
Mbabane
SWAZILAND
Johannesburg

Antananarivo

Maseru
LESOTHO
Durban

REPUBLIC OF SOUTH AFRICA

Cape Town

SOUTHERN OCEAN

N

Fact box

	population:	886 727 000 people
	largest country:	Sudan 2 505 772km²
	country with most people:	Nigeria 131 529 000
	largest city:	Lagos, Nigeria 11 134 000

Key

	colours show countries
MALI	country names are labelled like this
	capital cities
•	other important cities

Compare

Look at the size of the British Isles compared to Africa

Many countries in Africa have no sea coast. How many can you find on the map?

?

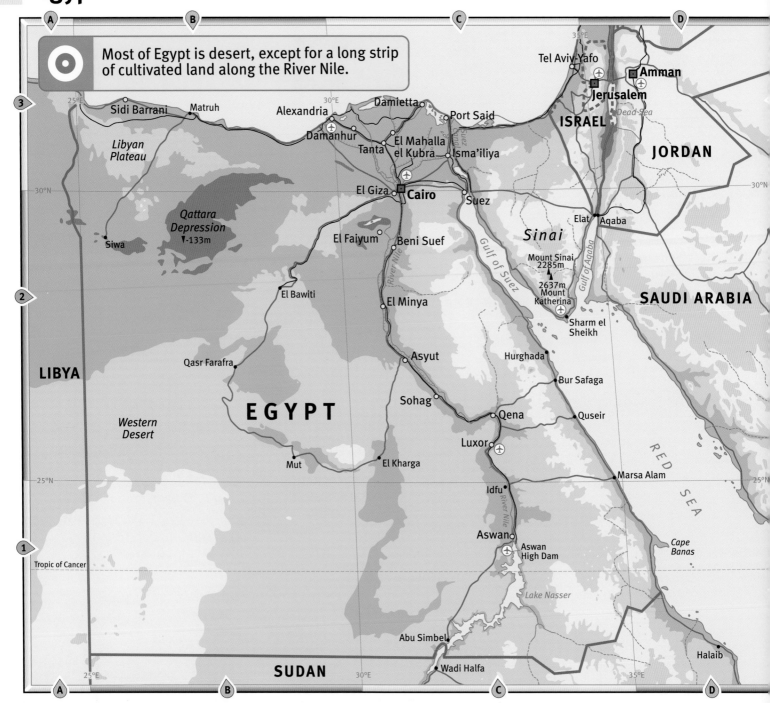

Most of Egypt is desert, except for a long strip of cultivated land along the River Nile.

LIBYA

Sidi Barrani
Matruh
Libyan Plateau
Siwa
Qattara Depression ▼-133m

Alexandria
Damietta
Port Said
Damanhur
Tanta
El Mahalla el Kubra
Isma'iliya
El Giza
Cairo
Suez
El Faiyum
Beni Suef

EGYPT

El Bawiti
El Minya
Qasr Farafra
Asyut
Western Desert
Sohag
Mut
El Kharga
Qena
Luxor
Idfu
Aswan
Aswan High Dam
Abu Simbel
Lake Nasser
Wadi Halfa

SUDAN

Tel Aviv-Yafo
Amman
Jerusalem
Dead Sea
ISRAEL
JORDAN
Elat
Aqaba
Sinai
Mount Sinai 2285m
2637m Mount Katherina
SAUDI ARABIA
Sharm el Sheikh
Hurghada
Bur Safaga
Quseir
Marsa Alam
Cape Banas
Halaib

RED SEA
Gulf of Suez
Gulf of Aqaba

25°E, 30°E, 35°E
30°N, 25°N
Tropic of Cancer
River Nile

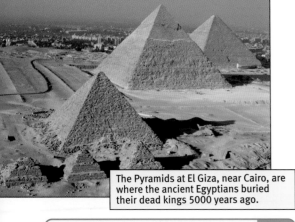

The Pyramids at El Giza, near Cairo, are where the ancient Egyptians buried their dead kings 5000 years ago.

The Aswan High Dam holds back the water of Lake Nasser and prevents the River Nile from flooding. Can you find the dam on the map?

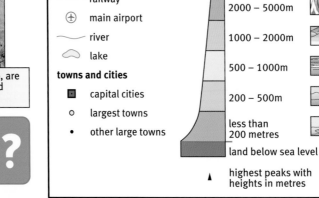

Key

— country boundary
--- disputed boundary
— motorway or main road
— railway
⊕ main airport
∼ river
⌒ lake

towns and cities
◼ capital cities
○ largest towns
• other large towns

land height
above sea level in metres

more than 5000m
2000 – 5000m
1000 – 2000m
500 – 1000m
200 – 500m
less than 200 metres
land below sea level
▲ highest peaks with heights in metres

Scale

One centimetre on the map represents 70 kilometres on the ground.

0   70   140   210km

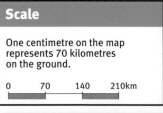

Locator

Egypt
East Africa

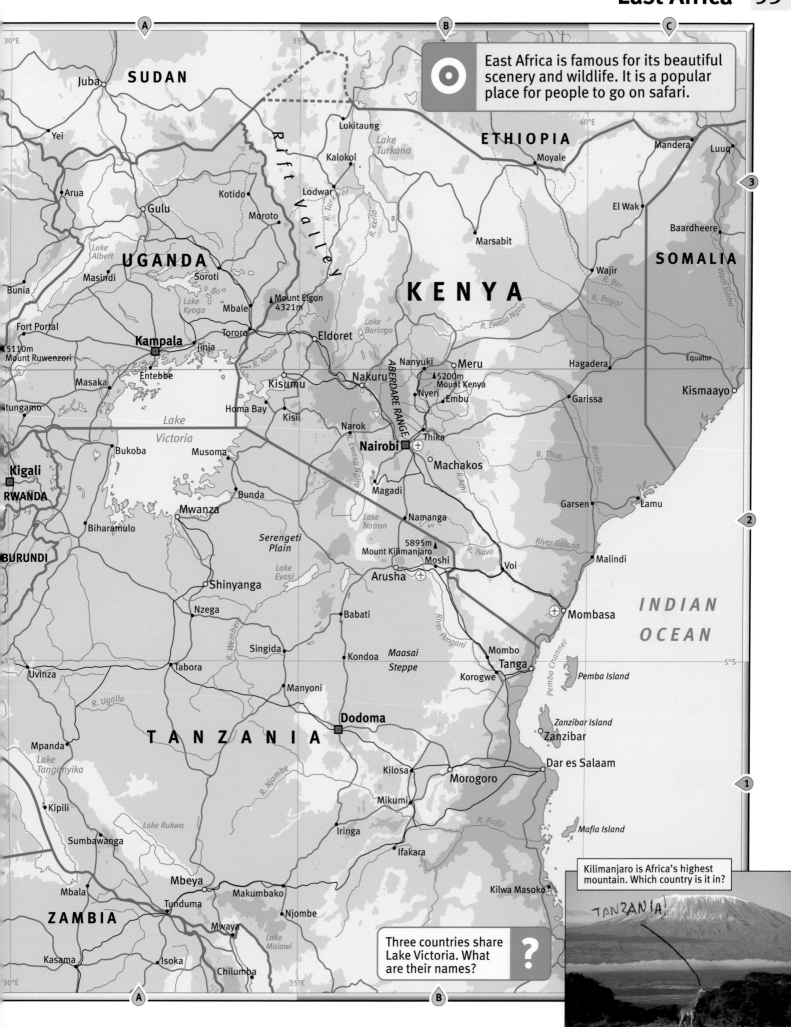

East Africa is famous for its beautiful scenery and wildlife. It is a popular place for people to go on safari.

SUDAN

Juba

Yei

Arua

Gulu

Kotido

Moroto

Lokitaung

Lake Turkana

Kalokol

Lodwar

R. Turkwel

R. Kerio

ETHIOPIA

Moyale

Mandera

Luuq

Marsabit

El Wak

Baardheere

UGANDA

Masindi

Bunia

Fort Portal

5110m Mount Ruwenzori

Lake Albert

Soroti

Lake Kyoga

Mbale

Mount Elgon 4321m

Tororo

Rift Valley

Wajir

SOMALIA

R. Bor

R. Bogai

Wadi Jubba

KENYA

Lake Baringo

Eldoret

R. Nzoia

Kampala

Jinja

Entebbe

Masaka

Kisumu

Nakuru

Nanyuki

Meru

5200m Mount Kenya

Nyeri

Embu

Hagadera

R. Ewaso Ngiro

Equator 0°

Kismaayo

Itungamo

Homa Bay

Kisii

Narok

ABERDARE RANGE

Thika

Garissa

Lake Victoria

Bukoba

Musoma

Nairobi

Machakos

R. Athi

R. Thua

River Tana

Kigali

RWANDA

Bunda

Magadi

Namanga

Garsen

Lamu

Mwanza

Lake Natron

Ewaso Ngiro

BURUNDI

Biharamulo

Serengeti Plain

River Galana

5895m Mount Kilimanjaro

Moshi

Voi

Malindi

INDIAN OCEAN

Shinyanga

Lake Eyasi

Arusha

Nzega

Babati

R. Tsavo

River Pangani

Mombasa

R. Wembere

Singida

Kondoa

Maasai Steppe

Mombo

Tanga

Uvinza

Tabora

Korogwe

Pemba Channel

Pemba Island

Manyoni

R. Ugalla

Dodoma

TANZANIA

Mpanda

Lake Tanganyika

R. Njombe

Kilosa

Morogoro

Dar es Salaam

Zanzibar Island

Zanzibar

Kipili

Mikumi

Mafia Island

Sumbawanga

Lake Rukwa

Iringa

R. Rufiji

Ifakara

Mbeya

Mbala

Makumbako

Njombe

Kilwa Masoko

Tunduma

ZAMBIA

Mwaya

Lake Malawi

Kasama

Isoka

Chilumba

TANZANIA!

Three countries share Lake Victoria. What are their names? **?**

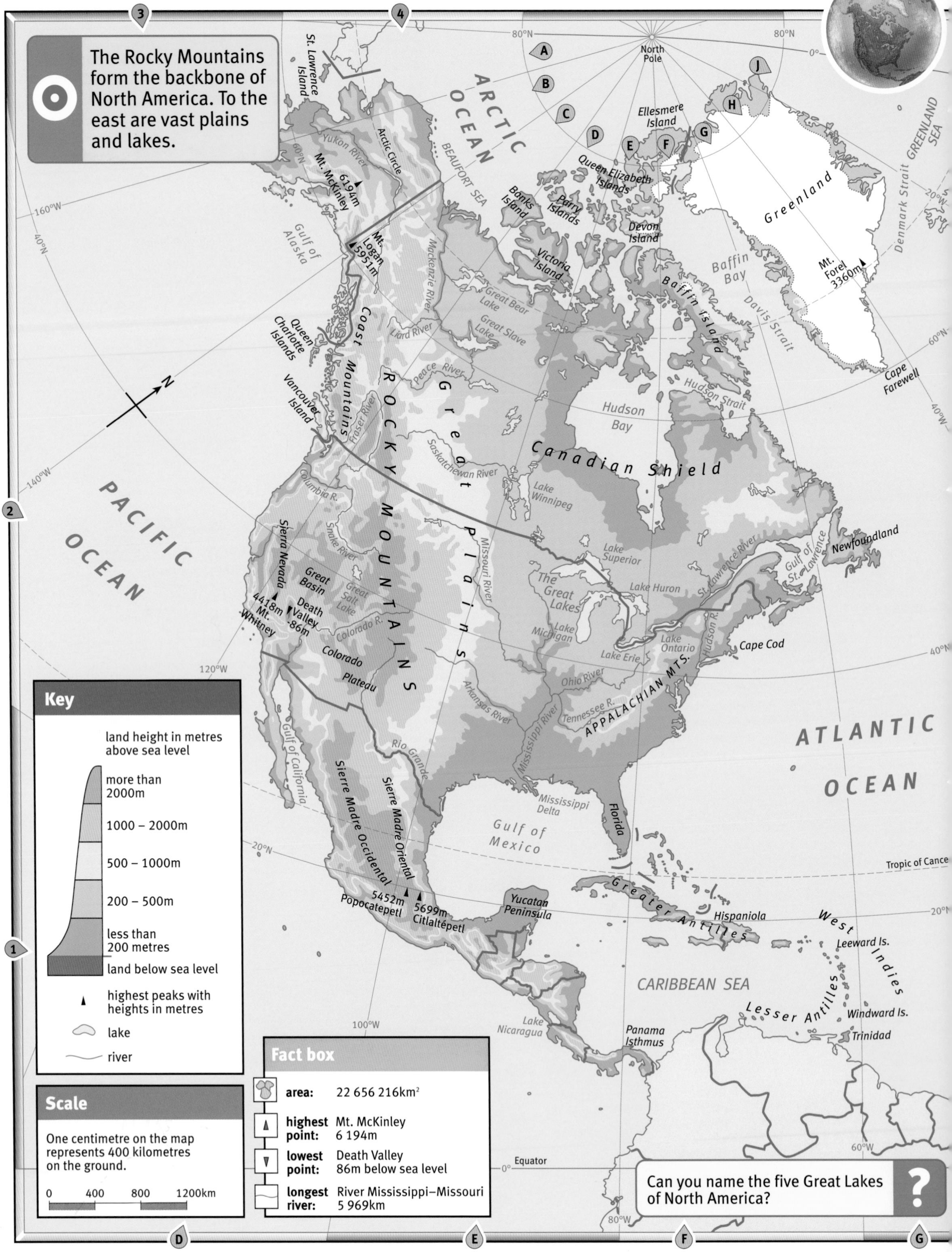
ARCTIC OCEAN
BEAUFORT SEA
North Pole
80°N
Ellesmere Island
Queen Elizabeth Islands
Parry Islands
Banks Island
Devon Island
Victoria Island
Baffin Bay
Baffin Island
Davis Strait
Greenland
Mt. Forel 3360m
GREENLAND SEA
Denmark Strait
Cape Farewell
Hudson Strait
Hudson Bay
Canadian Shield
St. Lawrence Island
Yukon River
Arctic Circle
Mt. McKinley 6194m
Gulf of Alaska
Mt. Logan 5951m
Mackenzie River
Great Bear Lake
Great Slave Lake
Liard River
Peace River
Queen Charlotte Islands
Coast Mountains
Vancouver Island
Fraser River
ROCKY MOUNTAINS
Great Plains
Saskatchewan River
Lake Winnipeg
PACIFIC OCEAN
Columbia R.
Snake River
Sierra Nevada
Great Basin
Great Salt Lake
Death Valley -86m
4418m Mt. Whitney
Colorado R.
Colorado Plateau
Missouri River
Lake Superior
The Great Lakes
Lake Huron
Lake Michigan
Lake Erie
Lake Ontario
St. Lawrence River
Gulf of St. Lawrence
Newfoundland
Hudson R.
Cape Cod
Ohio River
APPALACHIAN MTS.
Tennessee R.
Arkansas River
Mississippi River
Rio Grande
Gulf of California
Sierre Madre Occidental
Sierre Madre Oriental
Mississippi Delta
Florida
Gulf of Mexico
ATLANTIC OCEAN
Tropic of Cancer
5452m Popocatepetl
5699m Citlaltépetl
Yucatan Peninsula
Greater Antilles
Hispaniola
West Indies
Leeward Is.
CARIBBEAN SEA
Lesser Antilles
Windward Is.
Trinidad
Lake Nicaragua
Panama Isthmus
Equator
160°W
140°W
120°W
100°W
80°W
60°W
0°
20°W
40°N
60°N
20°N
40°W
1
2
3
4
A
B
C
D
E
F
G
H
J

The Rocky Mountains form the backbone of North America. To the east are vast plains and lakes.

Key

land height in metres above sea level

- more than 2000m
- 1000 – 2000m
- 500 – 1000m
- 200 – 500m
- less than 200 metres
- land below sea level
- highest peaks with heights in metres
- lake
- river

Scale

One centimetre on the map represents 400 kilometres on the ground.

0 400 800 1200km

Fact box

area:	22 656 216km²
highest point:	Mt. McKinley 6 194m
lowest point:	Death Valley 86m below sea level
longest river:	River Mississippi–Missouri 5 969km

Can you name the five Great Lakes of North America?

Oblique Mercator Projection

ARCTIC OCEAN

Arctic Circle

60°N

A
B
C
D
E
F
G

⊙ The large countries of Canada, the United States and Mexico make up most of North America.

80°N

USA
ALASKA

Anchorage

GREENLAND
(Denmark)

■ Nuuk

60°N

40°W

C A N A D A

Vancouver
Seattle
Portland
Edmonton
Calgary

Winnipeg

PACIFIC OCEAN

San Francisco
• Sacramento
Salt Lake City
Minneapolis
Québec
Ottawa
Montréal
St-Pierre & Miquelon
(France)
Halifax

Los Angeles
San Diego
Denver
Kansas City
Chicago
Detroit
Toronto
Pittsburgh
New York
Boston

U N I T E D   S T A T E S   O F   A M E R I C A

• Phoenix

St Louis
Washington D.C.
Philadelphia

40°N

Tropic of Cancer

• Dallas
• Atlanta

ATLANTIC OCEAN

Houston

Bermuda
(UK)

2

Monterrey

New Orleans

Gulf of Mexico

Miami

THE BAHAMAS
■ Nassau

Fact box

👤	population:	511 166 000 people
🗺	largest country:	Canada 9 970 601km²
👪	country with most people:	USA 298 213 000
■	largest city:	Mexico City, Mexico 18 934 000

Guadalajara

MEXICO

■ Mexico City
• Puebla

Havana

CUBA

DOMINICAN REPUBLIC

PUERTO RICO
(USA)

ST. KITTS AND NEVIS

Belmopan
GUATEMALA
BELIZE
Guatemala City
HONDURAS
Kingston
JAMAICA
HAITI
Port-au-Prince
Santo Domingo
■ San Juan

ANTIGUA & BARBUDA

DOMINICA

San Salvador
Tegucigalpa
CARIBBEAN SEA
ST. VINCENT & THE GRENADINES
ST. LUCIA
BARBADOS

EL SALVADOR
NICARAGUA
Managua
GRENADA
Port of Spain

San José
COSTA RICA
Panama City
PANAMA
TRINIDAD & TOBAGO

1

Key

⬚ colours show countries

CUBA country names are labelled like this

■ capital cities

• other important cities

Compare

Look at the size of the British Isles compared to North America

Equator 0°

VENEZUELA
GUYANA
COLOMBIA

The capital of the USA is **Washington D.C.** Can you find out what **D.C.** stands for? ❓

D
E
F
G

© Oxford University Press

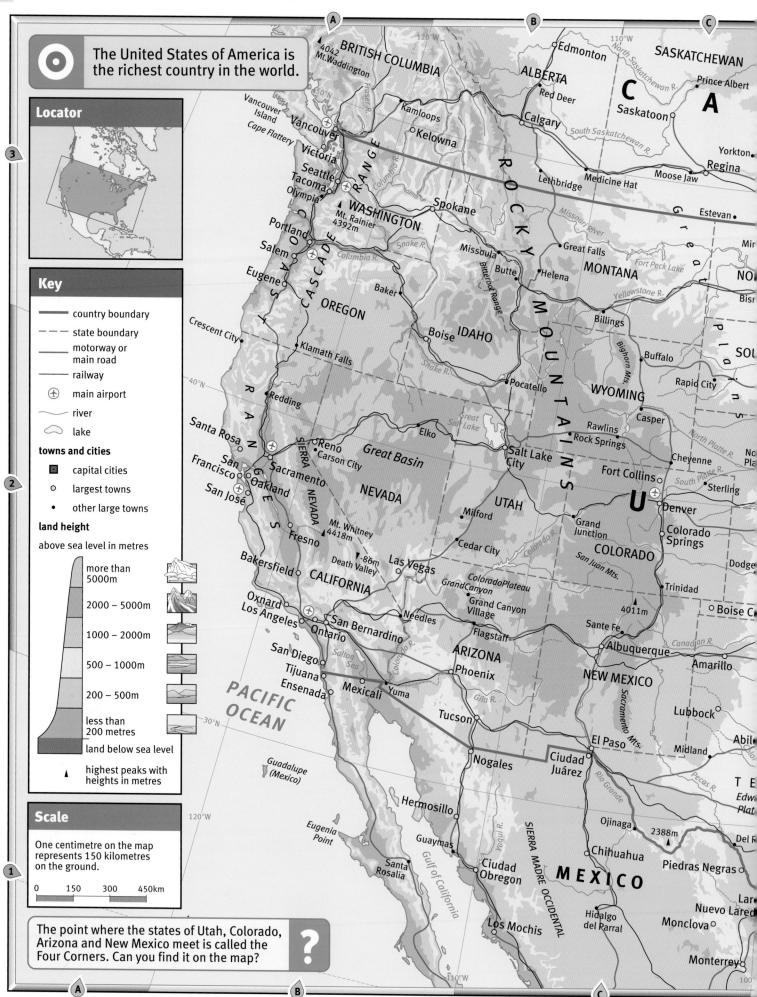

Locator

Key

	country boundary
	state boundary
	motorway or main road
	railway
✈	main airport
	river
	lake

towns and cities

■	capital cities
○	largest towns
•	other large towns

land height

above sea level in metres

| more than 5000m |
| 2000 – 5000m |
| 1000 – 2000m |
| 500 – 1000m |
| 200 – 500m |
| less than 200 metres |
| land below sea level |
| ▲ | highest peaks with heights in metres |

Scale

One centimetre on the map represents 150 kilometres on the ground.

0   150   300   450km

The point where the states of Utah, Colorado, Arizona and New Mexico meet is called the Four Corners. Can you find it on the map?

?

The United States of America is the richest country in the world.

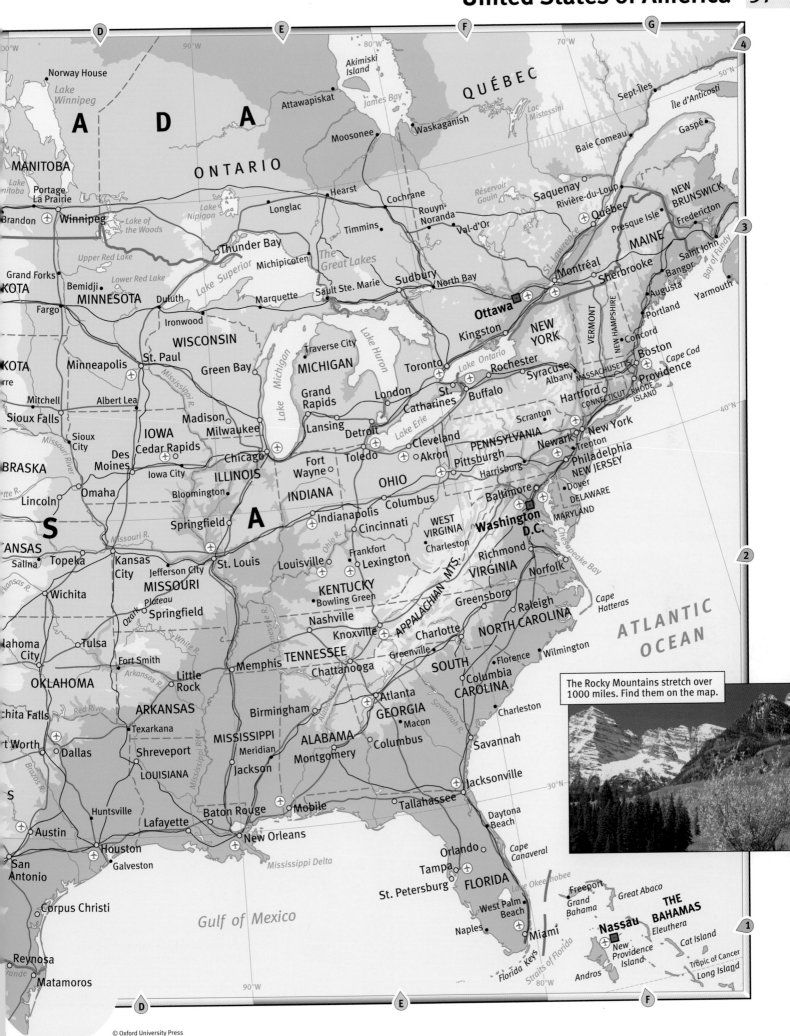

The Rocky Mountains stretch over 1000 miles. Find them on the map.

The Andes are the longest mountain range in the world and stretch the whole length of South America.

Key

land height in metres above sea level

more than 2000m

1000 – 2000m

500 – 1000m

200 – 500m

less than 200 metres

land below sea level

▲ highest peaks with heights in metres

lake

river

Fact box

area:	17 867 239km²	
highest point:	Aconcagua	6 960m
lowest point:	Valdés Peninsula	40m below sea level
longest river:	River Amazon	6 516km

Scale

One centimetre on the map represents 350 kilometres on the ground.

0   350   700   850km

Can you find out which famous scientist studied plants and animals on the Galapagos Islands in 1835?

ATLANTIC OCEAN

PACIFIC OCEAN

ATLANTIC OCEAN

SOUTHERN OCEAN

Cocos Islands
Galapagos Islands
Equator
Cotopaxi 5896m
Chimborazo 6310m
Lake Maracaibo
Llanos
River Orinoco
GUIANA HIGHLANDS
Mt. Roraima 2810m
Rocas Island
River Magdalena
A N D E S
River Negro
River Amazon
River Amazon
River Ucayali
Amazon Basin
Selvas
River Madeira
River Tapajos
River Tocantins
River São Francisco
Mato Grosso
BRAZILIAN HIGHLANDS
Lake Titicaca
Lake Poopo
Atacama Desert
River Pilcomayo
River Paraguay
Gran Chaco
6908m Ojos del Salado
Aconcagua 6960m
Juan Fernández Islands
River Paraná
River Uruguay
Pampas
Tropic of Capricorn
R. Colorado
R. Negro
Rio de la Plata
Patagonia
Valdés Peninsula
Chiloé Island
Falkland Islands
Tierra del Fuego
Cape Horn
South Georgia

N

80°W   60°W   40°W   20°W

40°W

0°
20°S
40°S

CARIBBEAN SEA

Barranquilla

Caracas

Maracaibo

Valencia

VENEZUELA

COSTA RICA

PANAMA

Medellin

Georgetown

Paramaribo

GUYANA

SURINAME

Cayenne

French Guiana
(France)

Cali

Bogota

COLOMBIA

Quito

ECUADOR

Guayaquil

Equator

*Galapagos Islands
(Ecuador)*

Iquitos

Belem

Manaus

Fortaleza

*Rocas Island
(Brazil)*

Trujillo

PERU

B   R   A   Z   I   L

Recife

Lima

BOLIVIA

Salvador

Arequipa

La Paz

Santa
Cruz

Brásília

Sucre

Belo
Horizonte

Antofagasta

PARAGUAY

Rio de
Janeiro

São Paulo

Asunción

Curitiba

Tropic of Capricorn

Porto Alegre

PACIFIC

OCEAN

Cordoba

Rosario

URUGUAY

Santiago

Buenos Aires

Montevideo

*Juan Fernandez Is.
(Chile)*

ARGENTINA

Mar del Plata

Concepcion

ATLANTIC

OCEAN

ATLANTIC
OCEAN

N

Brazilians speak Portuguese. Most other
South Americans speak Spanish.

Fact box

population:	370 056 000 people	
largest country:	Brazil 8 547 361km²	
country with most people:	Brazil 186 405 000	
largest city:	São Paulo 19 591 000	

Key

	colours show countries
PERU	country names are labelled like this
◙	capital cities
•	other important cities

Stanley

*Falkland Islands
(UK)*

Punta Arenas

*South Georgia
(UK)*

SOUTHERN   OCEAN

South America contains the world's longest,
thinnest country. Can you name it?

?

Compare

Look at the size of the British
Isles compared to
South America

The Amazon rain forest contains half of all known plants and animals on Earth.

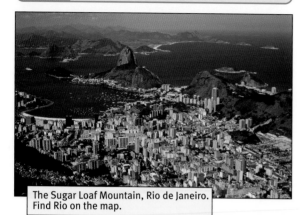

The Sugar Loaf Mountain, Rio de Janeiro. Find Rio on the map.

The capital of Brazil was built as a brand new city in 1960. Can you name it? **?**

Key

——	country boundary	
- - -	disputed boundary	
——	motorway or main road	
—	railway	
⊕	main airport	
〰	river	
⌒	lake	

land height

above sea level in metres

more than 5000m	
2000 – 5000m	
1000 – 2000m	
500 – 1000m	
200 – 500m	
less than 200 metres	
land below sea level	

▲ highest peaks with heights in metres

towns and cities

■	capital cities
○	largest towns
•	other large towns

Scale

One centimetre on the map represents 160 kilometres on the ground.

0   160   320   480km

Locator

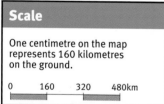

60°W

D
50°W
E
40°W
F

GUYANA SURINAME French Guiana (France)

Boa Vista

Serra Tumucumaque

Barcelos

River Branco

Balbina Reservoir

Macapa

Ilha de Marajo

Mouths of the Amazon

River Amazon

ATLANTIC OCEAN

Equator 0°

5

Manaus

Manacapuru

Coari

R. Xingu

Santarem

Cameta

Belem

Braganca

São Luis

Parnaiba

4

River Madeira

River Irirí

Itaituba

Altamira

Tucurui

Bacabal

Codo

Caxias

Sobral

Fortaleza

Porto Velho

River Tapajos

River Teles Pires

Maraba

Imperatriz

Teresina

Barra do Corda

Mossoro

Natal

Ariquemes

River Aripuana

Araguaina

River Araguaia

Juazeiro do Norte

Campina Grande

Joao Pessoa

Recife

Caruaru

River Guapore

B **R** **A** **Z**

Petrolina

Maceio

10°S

Barreiras

River Tocantins

River Parnaiba

Diamantina

Feira de Santana

Alagoinhas

Salvador

I **L**

River São Francisco

Chapada

Vitoria da Conquista

Jequie

Ilheus

3

BOLIVIA

Santa Cruz

Sucre

Trinidad

Mato Grosso

Cuiaba

Caceres

Rondonopolis

Corumba

Anapolis

Goiania

Rio Verde

Brasilia

Montes Claros

BRAZILIAN

HIGHLANDS

River Paranaiba

Uberlandia

Mount Itambe 2033m

Teofilo Otoni

Governador Valadares

Linhares

Caratinga

Vitoria

Tarija

Gran Chaco

Sa. de Maracaju

Campo Grande

São Jose do Rio Preto

Uberaba

Ribeirao Preto

Belo Horizonte

Barbacena

River Jequitinhonha

Campos

20°S

Pedro Juan Caballero

Dourados

Araraquara

Bauru

Juiz de Fora

San Salvador de Jujuy

River Pilcomayo

PARAGUAY

Maringa

Campinas

Nova Iguacu

Rio de Janeiro

Salta

River Bermejo

Asuncion

Foz do Iguacu

Ponta Grossa

São Paulo

Santo Andre

Santos

Tropic of Capricorn

Formosa

River Paraguay

River Parana

Curitiba

Paranagua

ATLANTIC OCEAN

2

San Miguel de Tucuman

Resistencia

Corrientes

Posadas

Itajai

Florianopolis

ARGENTINA

Santiago del Estero

River Uruguay

Passo Fundo

Caxias do Sul

S. Grandes

River Salado

Uruguaiana

Santa Maria

Porto Alegre

30°S

Cordoba

Santa Fe

Parana

Concordia

URUGUAY

Lagoa dos Patos

Pelotas

Rio Grande

60°W

C

D

50°W

E

40°W

F

30°S

© Oxford University Press

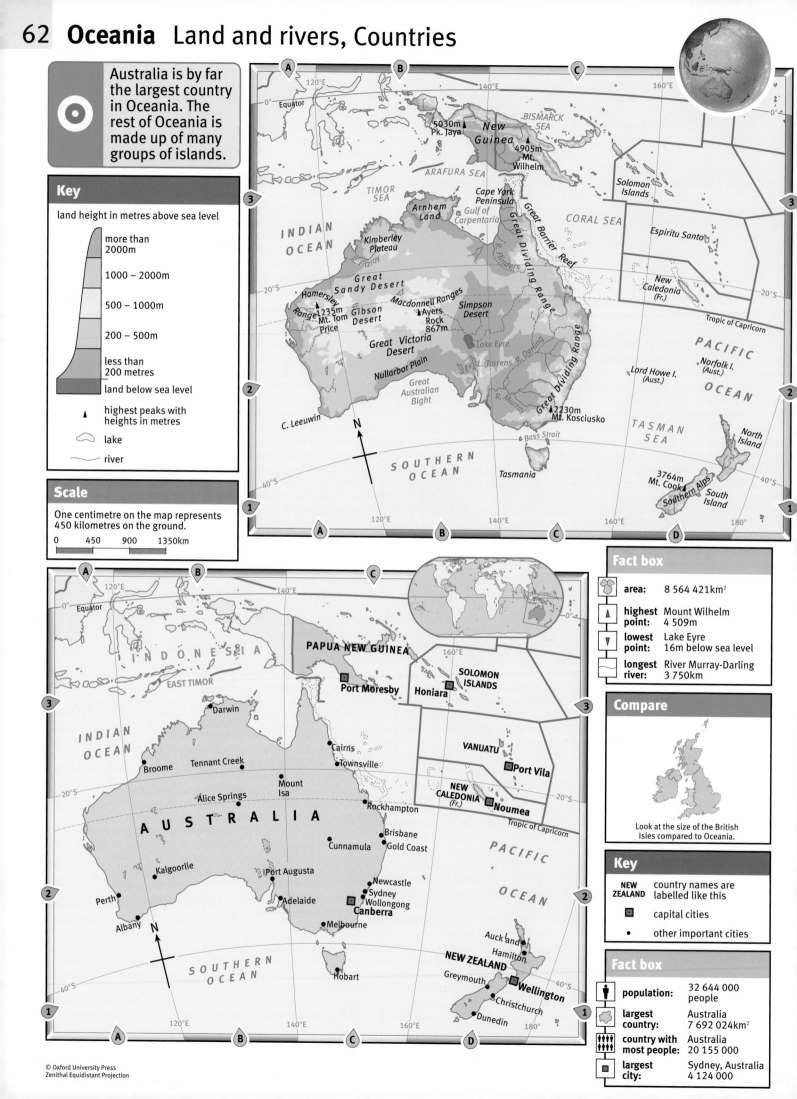

Australia is by far the largest country in Oceania. The rest of Oceania is made up of many groups of islands.

Key

land height in metres above sea level

more than 2000m

1000 – 2000m

500 – 1000m

200 – 500m

less than 200 metres

land below sea level

▲ highest peaks with heights in metres

lake

river

Scale

One centimetre on the map represents 450 kilometres on the ground.

0   450   900   1350km

Fact box

	area:	8 564 421km²
▲	highest point:	Mount Wilhelm 4 509m
▼	lowest point:	Lake Eyre 16m below sea level
	longest river:	River Murray-Darling 3 750km

Compare

Look at the size of the British Isles compared to Oceania.

Key

NEW ZEALAND country names are labelled like this

▪ capital cities

• other important cities

Fact box

	population:	32 644 000 people
	largest country:	Australia 7 692 024km²
	country with most people:	Australia 20 155 000
	largest city:	Sydney, Australia 4 124 000

The Arctic Ocean is mostly covered with frozen water.

Key

ice cap

sea covered by ice all year

▲ highest peaks with heights in metres

⊕ position of magnetic north in 2008

■ capital cities

Fact box

area: 14 200 000km²

depth of the ocean at the North Pole: 4 087m

Compare

Look at the size of the British Isles compared to the Arctic Ocean and Antarctica

Arctic Ocean map

BERING SEA
Bering Strait
USA
RUSSIAN FEDERATION (RUSSIA)
120°W
60°N
180°
60°E
120°E
CANADA
BEAUFORT SEA
80°N
ARCTIC
⊕
North Pole
OCEAN
Baffin Bay
Novaya Zemlya
Spitsbergen
80°N
BARENTS SEA
GREENLAND (Denmark)
Nuuk ■
Mount Forel ▲3360m
Prime Meridian
60°W
Arctic Circle
Reykjavik ■ ICELAND
NORWAY
SWEDEN
FINLAND
Oslo ■
Stockholm ■
Helsinki ■

Antarctica

Antarctica is always cold. The environment of the whole continent is protected.

Antarctica map

SOUTHERN OCEAN
0°
Antarctic Circle
South Orkney Islands P
SOUTHERN OCEAN
60°E
120°E
WEDDELL SEA
Queen Maud Land
South Shetland Islands
Larsen Ice Shelf
Antarctic Peninsula
Filchner Ice Shelf
Ronne Ice Shelf
Lambert Glacier
Prime Meridian
Mount Menzies ▲ 3355m
BELLINGSHAUSEN SEA
60°W
Vinson Massif ▲ 4897m
Ellsworth Land
South Pole
80°S
Wilkes Land
Marie-Byrd Land
Ross Ice Shelf
Mount Kirkpatrick ▲ 4528m
Mount Markham ▲ 4351m
AMUNDSEN SEA
McMurdo P
Mount Erebus ▲ 3743m
ROSS SEA
120°W
120°E
60°S
180°
SOUTHERN OCEAN

Key

ice cap

sea covered by ice all year

▲ highest peaks with heights in metres

⊕ position of magnetic south in 2008

P research station

Fact box

area: 13 340 000km²

highest point: Vinson Massif 4 897m

largest settlement: McMurdo Research Station. 1 200 scientists live there in summer and 200 in winter.

Scale

One centimetre on the map represents 500 kilometres on the ground.

0   500   1000   1500km

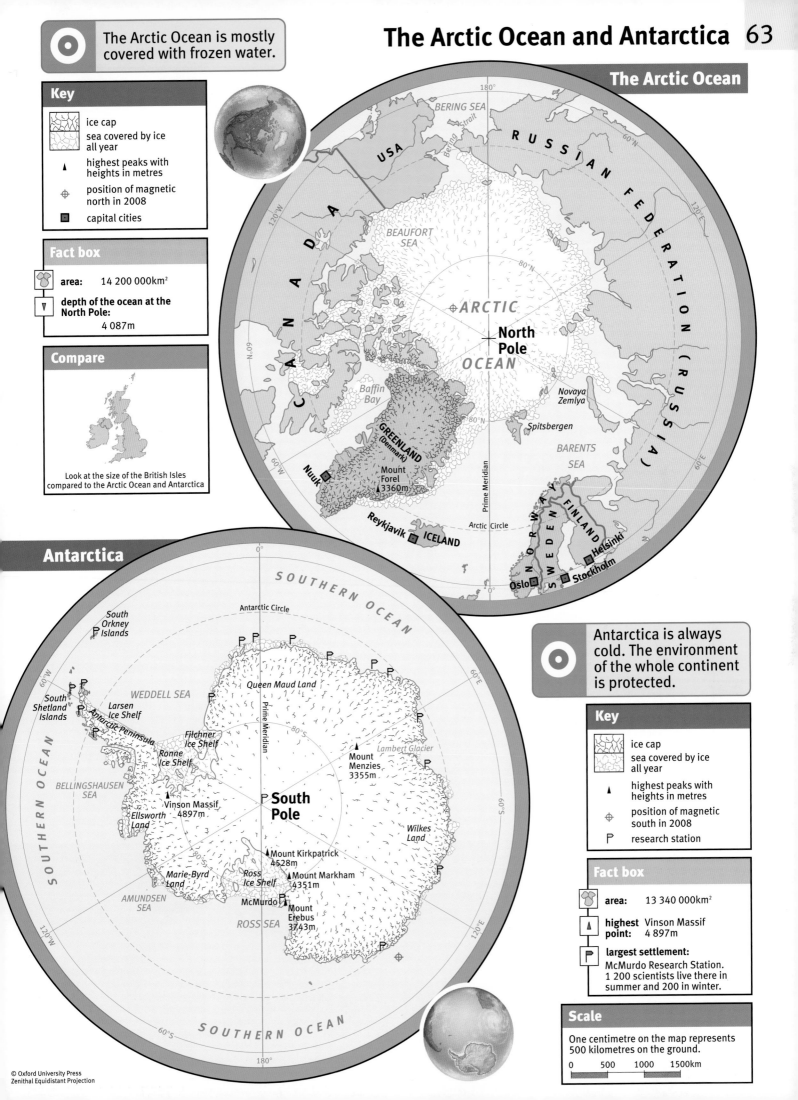

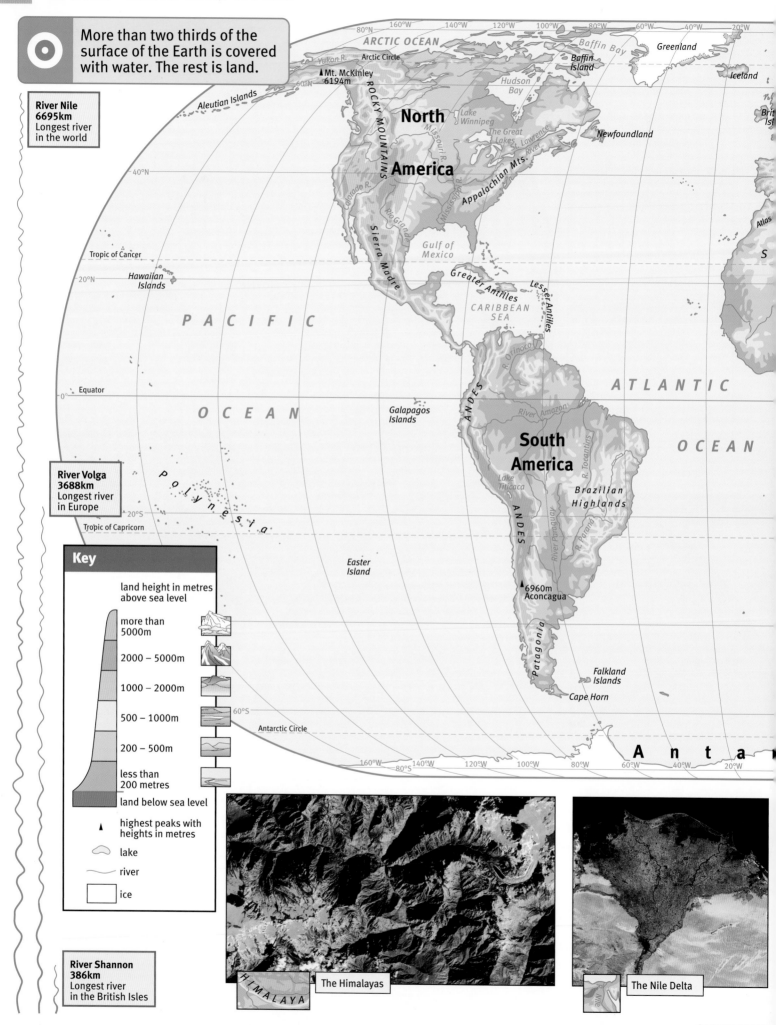

More than two thirds of the surface of the Earth is covered with water. The rest is land.

**River Nile
6695km**
Longest river
in the world

**River Volga
3688km**
Longest river
in Europe

**River Shannon
386km**
Longest river
in the British Isles

Key

land height in metres
above sea level

more than
5000m

2000 – 5000m

1000 – 2000m

500 – 1000m

200 – 500m

less than
200 metres

land below sea level

▲ highest peaks with
heights in metres

lake

river

ice

The Himalayas

The Nile Delta

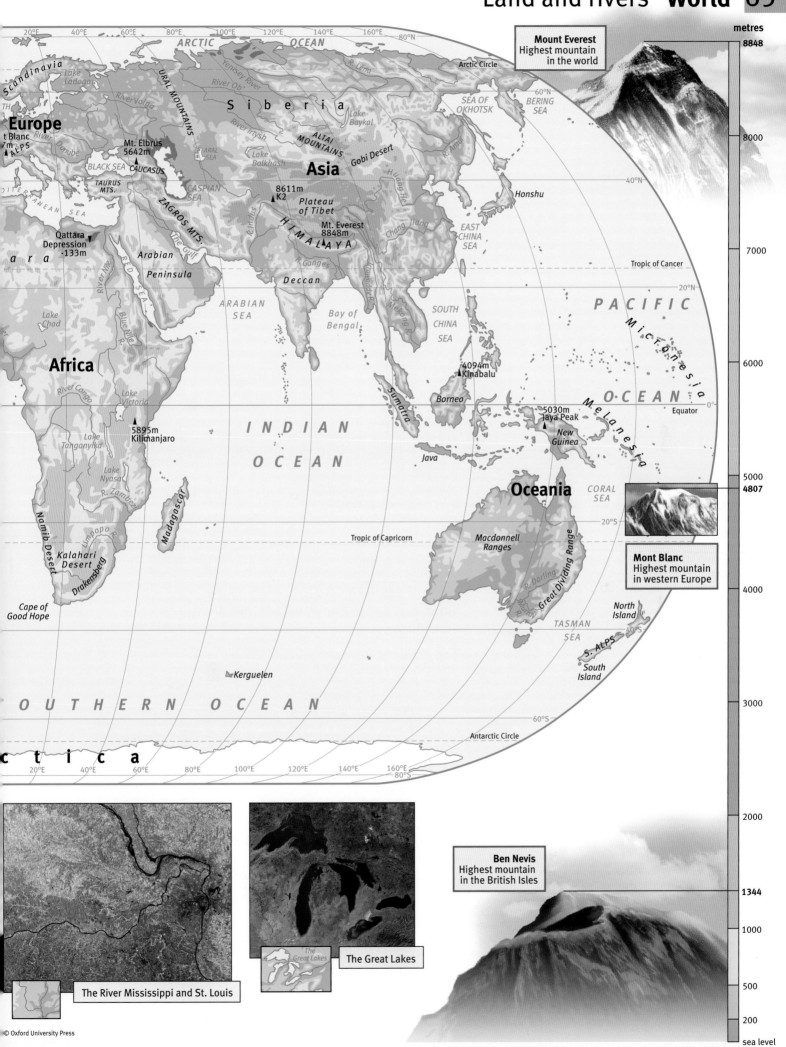

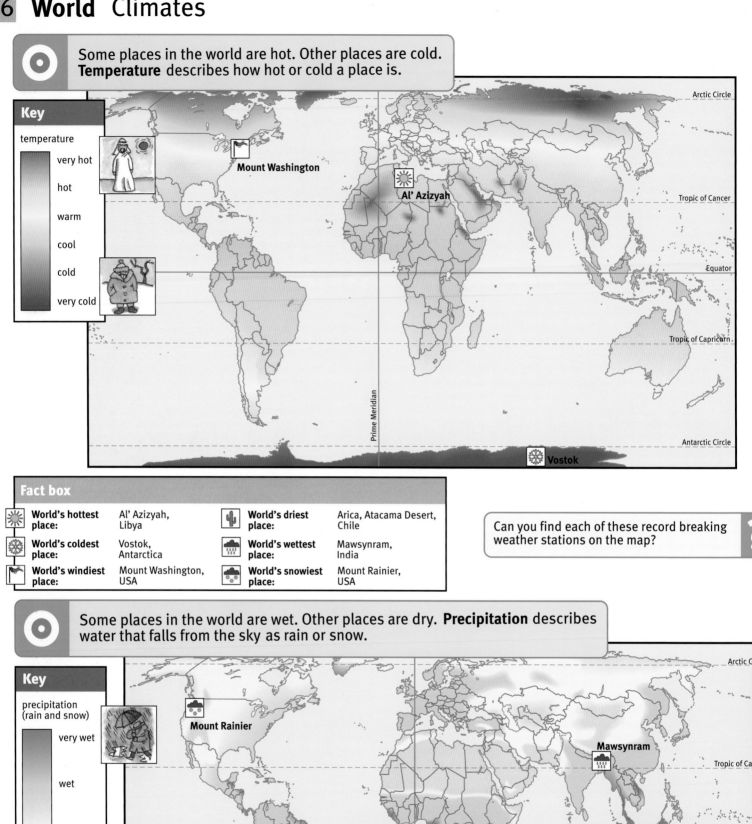

Some places in the world are hot. Other places are cold. **Temperature** describes how hot or cold a place is.

Key

temperature

very hot
hot
warm
cool
cold
very cold

Mount Washington

Al' Azizyah

Vostok

Arctic Circle
Tropic of Cancer
Equator
Tropic of Capricorn
Prime Meridian
Antarctic Circle

Fact box

	World's hottest place:	Al' Azizyah, Libya		World's driest place:	Arica, Atacama Desert, Chile
	World's coldest place:	Vostok, Antarctica		World's wettest place:	Mawsynram, India
	World's windiest place:	Mount Washington, USA		World's snowiest place:	Mount Rainier, USA

Can you find each of these record breaking weather stations on the map?

Some places in the world are wet. Other places are dry. **Precipitation** describes water that falls from the sky as rain or snow.

Key

precipitation (rain and snow)

very wet

wet

dry

very dry

Mount Rainier

Mawsynram

Arica

Arctic Cir
Tropic of Can
Equa
Prime Meridian
Tropic of Capric
Antarctic Cir

Patterns of temperature and precipitation throughout the year create different types of climate.

Key

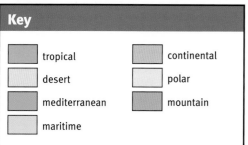

- tropical
- desert
- mediterranean
- maritime
- continental
- polar
- mountain

Tropical hot and wet
very hot and very wet all year

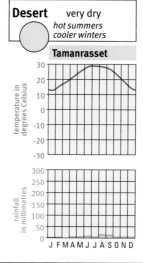

Castries

Desert very dry
hot summers cooler winters

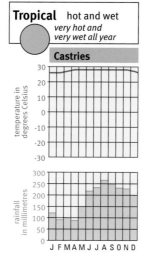

Tamanrasset

Mediterranean warm and wet
hot dry summers warm wet winters

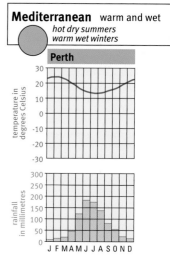

Perth

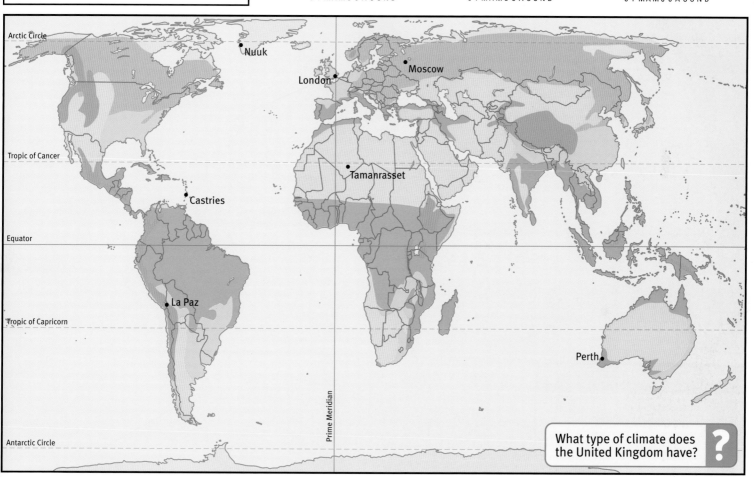

What type of climate does the United Kingdom have?

Maritime mild and wet
warm summers cool winters

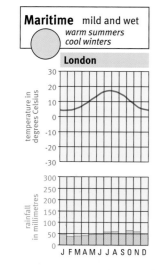

London

Continental cold and wet
warm summers cold winters

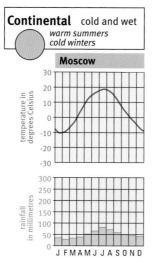

Moscow

Polar very cold and dry
very cold all year especially winters

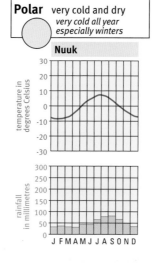

Nuuk

Mountain cold
cold because it is high. Heavy rain or snow

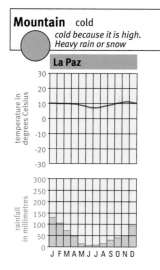

La Paz

© Oxford University Press

Each of the major world environments shown on the map has its own special climate, plant life and animals. Most natural environments have been influenced by people.

deciduous forest

coniferous forest

tropical forest

ARCTIC OCEAN

Arctic Circle

Tropic of Cancer

PACIFIC

OCEAN

Equator

ATLANTIC

OCEAN

Tropic of Capricorn

Antarctic Circle

Key

coniferous forest
trees have leaves all year

deciduous forest
trees drop their leaves in winter

tropical forest
tall trees growing close together

savannah
tall grass and scattered trees

temperate grassland
prairies, steppes, pampas and veld

semi desert
short grass and small dry bushes

desert
sand and stones with few plants

tundra
moss and bog with some short trees

ice
no plants

mountains
thin soils and steep slopes

desert

semi desert

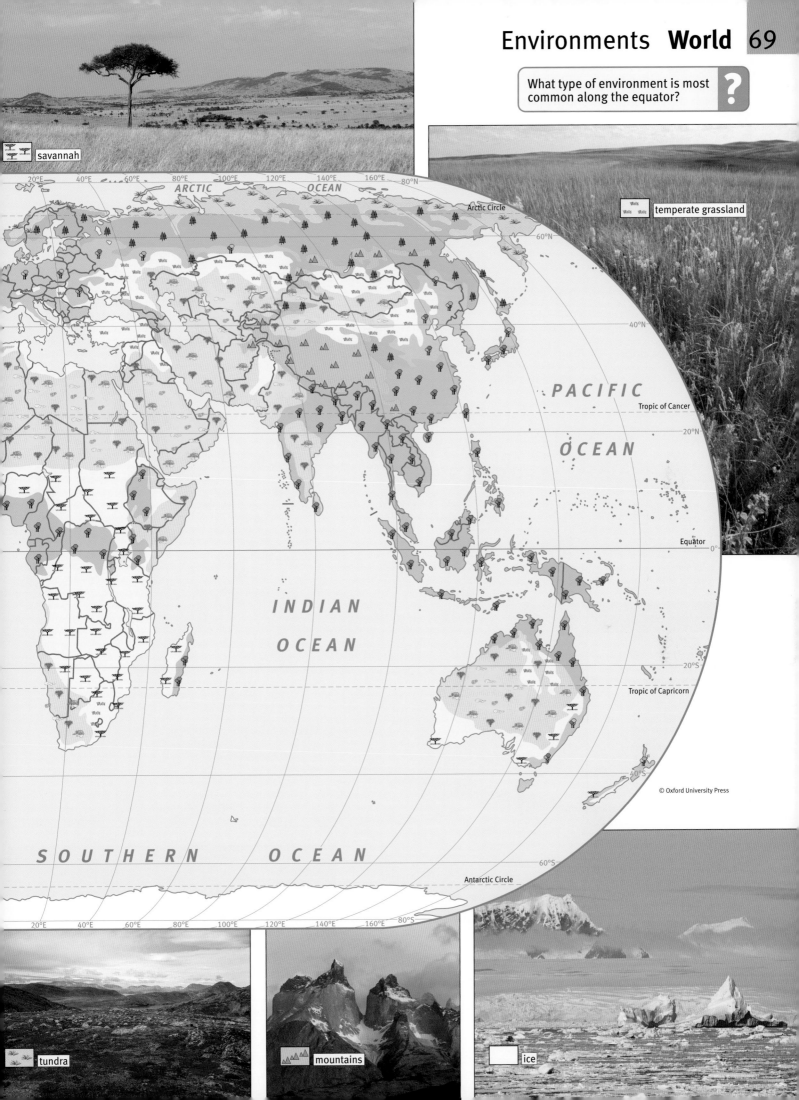

What type of environment is most common along the equator?

savannah

temperate grassland

ARCTIC OCEAN

Arctic Circle

60°N

40°N

PACIFIC

Tropic of Cancer

OCEAN

20°N

Equator 0°

INDIAN

OCEAN

20°S

Tropic of Capricorn

40°S

SOUTHERN OCEAN

60°S

Antarctic Circle

80°S

© Oxford University Press

tundra

mountains

ice

People have damaged the environment in many parts of the world. Cutting down forests and burning fossil fuels affects the Earth's atmosphere and can cause **climate change**.

Key

- tropical rain forest
- areas where rain forest has been cut down
- desert
- areas that are becoming desert
- areas most affected by air pollution
- sea areas most affected by oil pollution
- areas where ice is melting

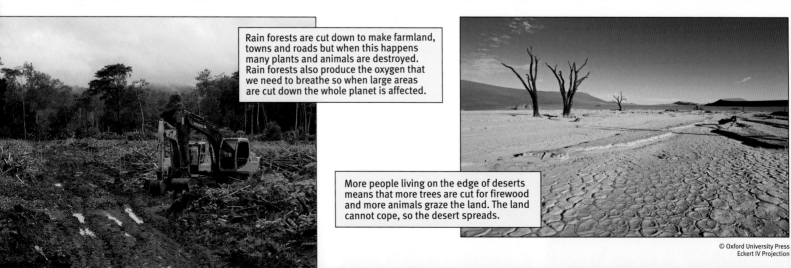

Rain forests are cut down to make farmland, towns and roads but when this happens many plants and animals are destroyed. Rain forests also produce the oxygen that we need to breathe so when large areas are cut down the whole planet is affected.

More people living on the edge of deserts means that more trees are cut for firewood and more animals graze the land. The land cannot cope, so the desert spreads.

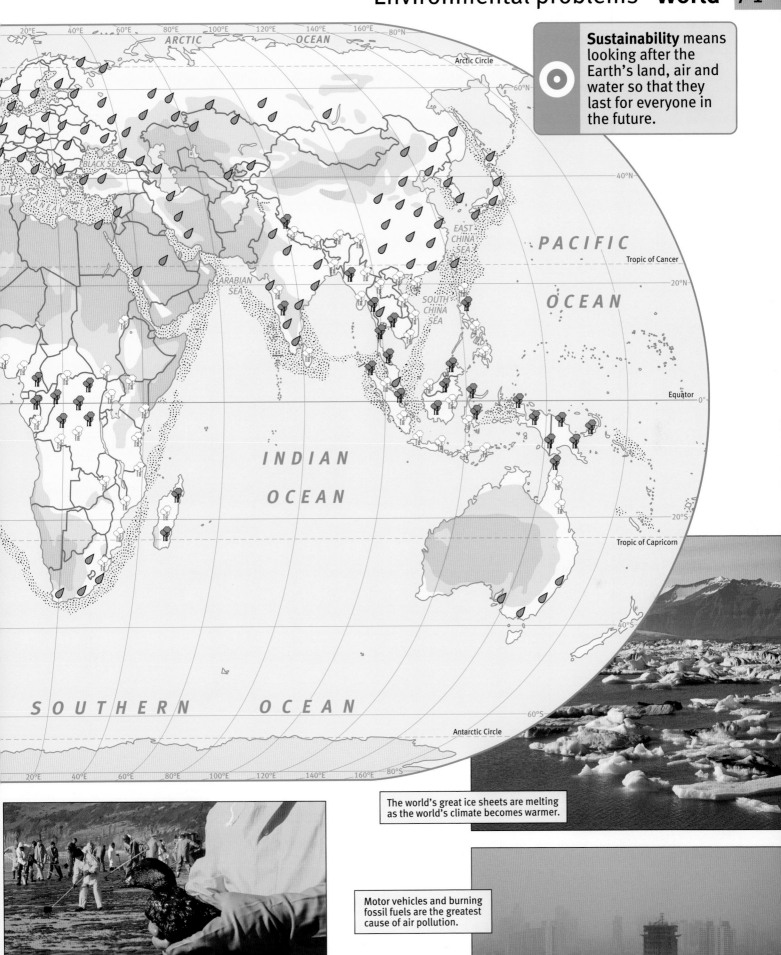

Sustainability means looking after the Earth's land, air and water so that they last for everyone in the future.

The world's great ice sheets are melting as the world's climate becomes warmer.

Motor vehicles and burning fossil fuels are the greatest cause of air pollution.

Oil spilt from ships and oil rigs can damage beaches and wildlife. Birds with oil on their wings cannot fly.

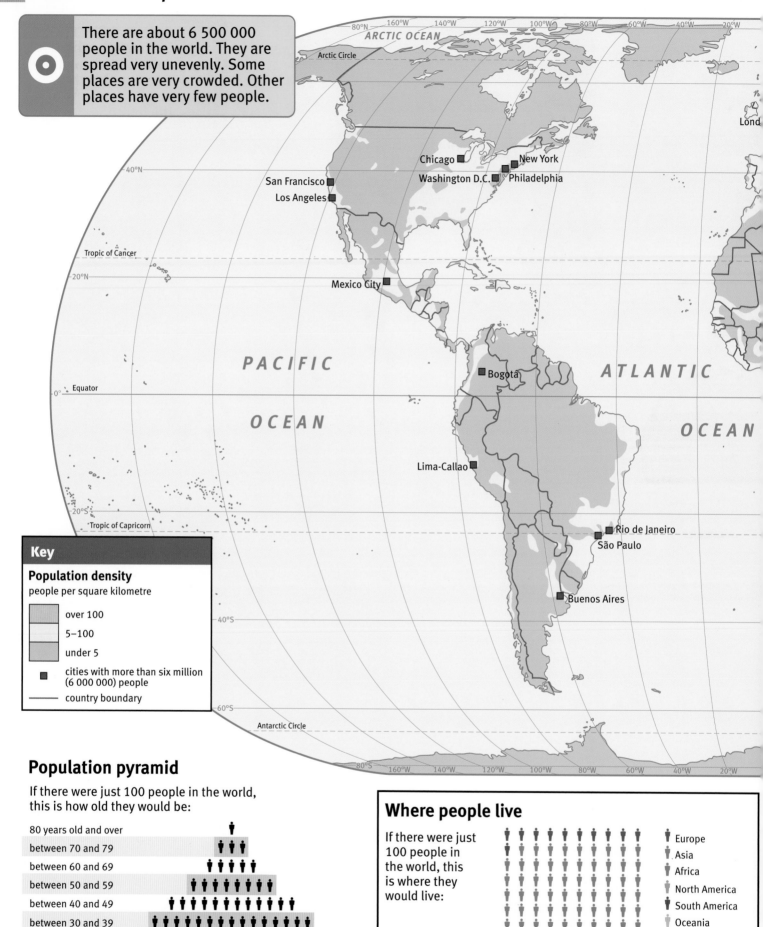

There are about 6 500 000 people in the world. They are spread very unevenly. Some places are very crowded. Other places have very few people.

Key

Population density
people per square kilometre

over 100

5–100

under 5

■ cities with more than six million (6 000 000) people

— country boundary

Cities labelled on map: Chicago, New York, Washington D.C., Philadelphia, San Francisco, Los Angeles, Mexico City, Bogotá, Lima-Callao, Rio de Janeiro, São Paulo, Buenos Aires, Lond...

ARCTIC OCEAN, Arctic Circle, Tropic of Cancer, Equator, Tropic of Capricorn, Antarctic Circle, PACIFIC OCEAN, ATLANTIC OCEAN

Population pyramid

If there were just 100 people in the world, this is how old they would be:

80 years old and over

between 70 and 79

between 60 and 69

between 50 and 59

between 40 and 49

between 30 and 39

between 20 and 29

between 10 and 19

9 years old and under

Where people live

If there were just 100 people in the world, this is where they would live:

Europe
Asia
Africa
North America
South America
Oceania

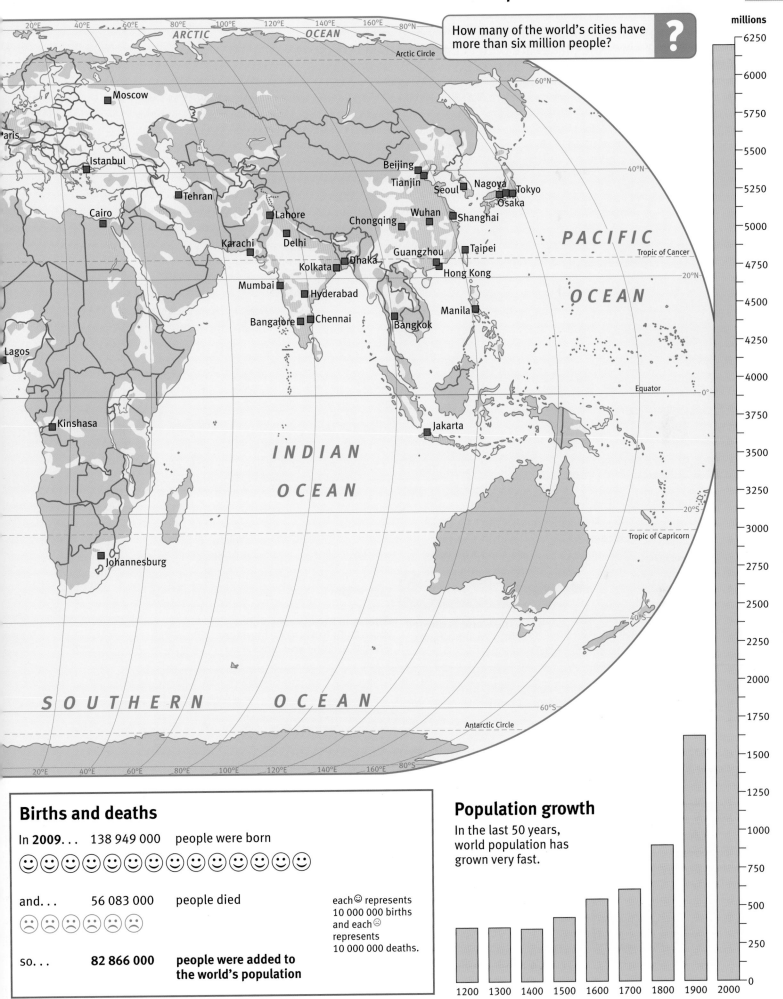

millions

How many of the world's cities have more than six million people? **?**

Births and deaths

In **2009**... 138 949 000 people were born

☺ ☺ ☺ ☺ ☺ ☺ ☺ ☺ ☺ ☺ ☺ ☺ ☺ ☺

and... 56 083 000 people died

☹ ☹ ☹ ☹ ☹ ☹

each ☺ represents 10 000 000 births and each ☹ represents 10 000 000 deaths.

so... **82 866 000** **people were added to the world's population**

Population growth

In the last 50 years, world population has grown very fast.

1200 1300 1400 1500 1600 1700 1800 1900 2000

Travel and communication around the world are becoming faster but some places are better connected than others.

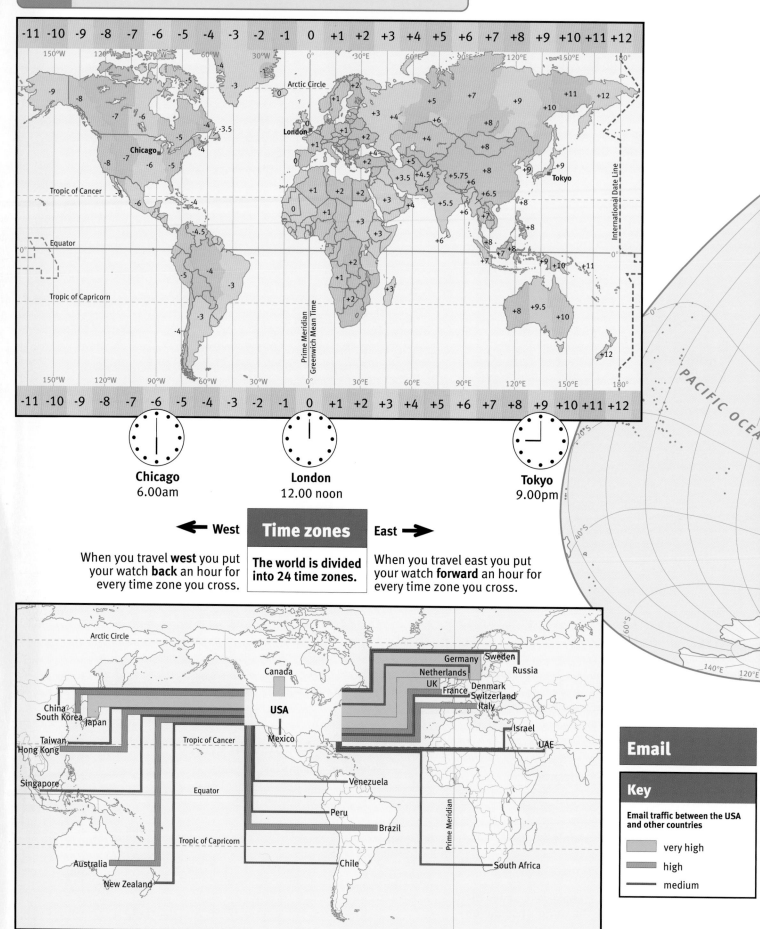

| -11 | -10 | -9 | -8 | -7 | -6 | -5 | -4 | -3 | -2 | -1 | 0 | +1 | +2 | +3 | +4 | +5 | +6 | +7 | +8 | +9 | +10 | +11 | +12 |

Chicago
6.00am

London
12.00 noon

Tokyo
9.00pm

← **West**

Time zones

East →

When you travel **west** you put your watch **back** an hour for every time zone you cross.

The world is divided into 24 time zones.

When you travel east you put your watch **forward** an hour for every time zone you cross.

Email

Key

Email traffic between the USA and other countries

very high
high
medium

© Oxford University Press
Gall Projection

The distance round the Earth at the Equator is 40 075 kilometres (24 846 miles)

20°N

Tokyo

ARCTIC
OCEAN
North Pole

Oceania

Sydney

San Francisco

North America

Seoul

Beijing

Taipei

Manila

Asia

Hong Kong

Bangkok

Singapore

Jakarta

Kuala Lumpur

13 15

13 15

23 15

15 00

Los Angeles

Las Vegas

Denver

Chicago

Toronto

Montreal

Houston

Dallas

Atlanta

New York

Miami

Honolulu

Mexico City

12 15

07 45

Moscow

London

Amsterdam
Frankfurt

Paris **Europe** Rome

Madrid

Athens

Cairo

INDIAN OCEAN

SOUTHERN OCEAN

15 15

Africa

12 30

ATLANTIC
OCEAN

South America

Buenos Aires

Johannesburg

20°E

40°S

South Pole

Antarctica

80°E 60°E 40°E

160°W

20°S

40°S

60°S

60°E

40°E

80°E

100°E

120°E

140°E

Flight connections

Key

— world's busiest air routes

⊕ world's largest airports

| 04 | 30 | flight time from London in hours and minutes

In 1950 it took a month to travel from the UK to Australia by sea. How long would a flight to Australia take today?

?

Tokyo

Beijing

Hong Kong

Singapore

Sydney

Mexico City

Los Angeles

New York

London

Paris

Dubai

Johannesburg

Buenos Aires

Distances

The chart shows flight distances from one city to another in kilometres*

Beijing											
19 307	**Buenos Aires**										
5 854	13 691	**Dubai**									
1 983	18 484	5 957	**Hong Kong**								
11 710	8 088	6 433	10 732	**Johannesburg**							
8 145	11 161	5 500	9 645	9 071	**London**						
10 081	9 871	13 414	11 678	16 676	8 774	**Los Angeles**					
12 468	7 468	14 341	14 162	14 585	8 936	2 484	**Mexico City**				
11 000	8 548	11 010	12 984	12 841	5 580	3 951	3 371	**New York**			
8 226	11 097	5 242	9 613	8 732	338	9 032	9 210	5 839	**Paris**		
4 468	15 904	5 841	2 661	8 860	10 871	14 146	16 630	15 533	10 758	**Singapore**	
8 949	11 800	12 056	7 374	11 040	16 992	12 073	12 969	15 989	16 962	6 300	**Sydney**
2 113	18 388	7 984	2 903	13 547	9 581	8 823	11 355	10 871	9 726	5 322	7 823	**Tokyo**

* To change kilometres to miles multiply by 0.62

Choose two countries. Using the information on these pages, can you say how your countries are the same and how they are different? **?**

Country area in square kilometres	**Population** estimated number of people in 2009 — represents 10 million people	**Family size** number of children in an average family — one child — **Years of life** number of years people can expect to live — represents 10 years	**Work** if there were 100 people in the country, this is where they would work — farms — factories — offices and services	**Rich and poor** the average amount each person spends in a year, converted into US dollars — $1000 — $500 — **Health** the number of doctors for every 10 000 people — one doctor

Australia
7 741 000km²

21 852 000 people

2 children

81 years

$37 250

25 doctors

Bangladesh
144 000km²

162 221 000 people

2.5 children

65 years

$1450

3 doctors

Brazil
8 547 000km²

191 481 000 people

2 children

73 years

$10 008

12 doctors

China
9 598 000km²

1 331 398 000 people

1.6 children

73 years

$6010

14 doctors

Ethiopia
1 104 000km²

82 825 000 people

5.3 children

53 years

$870

less than 1 doctor

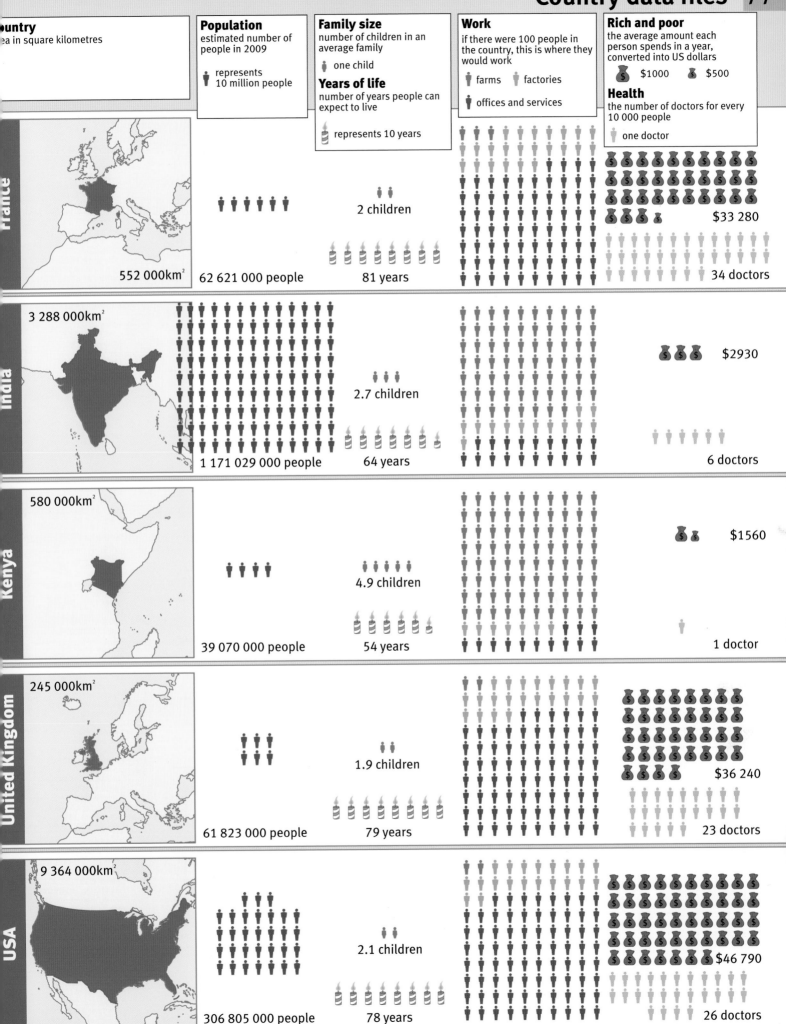

Country
ea in square kilometres

Population
estimated number of people in 2009

👤 represents 10 million people

Family size
number of children in an average family

👤 one child

Years of life
number of years people can expect to live

🕯 represents 10 years

Work
if there were 100 people in the country, this is where they would work

👤 farms 👤 factories

👤 offices and services

Rich and poor
the average amount each person spends in a year, converted into US dollars

💰 $1000 💰 $500

Health
the number of doctors for every 10 000 people

👤 one doctor

France
552 000km²
62 621 000 people
2 children
81 years
$33 280
34 doctors

India
3 288 000km²
1 171 029 000 people
2.7 children
64 years
$2930
6 doctors

Kenya
580 000km²
39 070 000 people
4.9 children
54 years
$1560
1 doctor

United Kingdom
245 000km²
61 823 000 people
1.9 children
79 years
$36 240
23 doctors

USA
9 364 000km²
306 805 000 people
2.1 children
78 years
$46 790
26 doctors

B — legend box:
name of place | grid code
Leeds **27** F3
page number

A

Aberdeen **23** G2
Aberystwyth **26** C2
Abidjan **51** A4
Abu Dhabi **46** A3
Abuja **51** B4
Accra **51** A4
Aconcagua *mountain* **58** B2
Adana **43** F2
Addis Ababa **51** C4
Adelaide **62** B2
Aden, Gulf of **44** B3
Adriatic Sea **42** D3
Aegean Sea **43** E2
Afghanistan **45** C4
Ahmadabad **47** C3
Albania **43** D3/E3
Albany **62** A2
Aldabra Islands **51** D3
Aldeburgh **29** F3
Alderney *island* **31** E1
Aleppo **45** A4
Aleutian Islands **54** A3
Alexandria **52** B3
Algeria **51** A5/B5
Algiers **51** B5
Alicante **42** B2
Alice Springs *town* **62** B2
Alloa **25** E3
Almaty **45** C5
Alps *mountains* **42** C3
Alaska, Gulf of **54** B3
Altai Mountains **48** C4
Amazon, River **60/61** C4/D4
Amlwch **26** C3
Amman **45** A4
Amsterdam **40** D2
Amur, River **49** F5
Anatolian Plateau **38** D1
Anchorage **55** B4
Andaman Islands **47** E2
Andaman Sea **44** D3
Andes *mountains* **58** B1/B4
Andorra **42** C3
Angara River **44** D5/E5
Anglesey *island* **26** C3
Angola **51** B3/C3
Angola Plateau **50** B3
Ankara **43** F2
Annan, River **25** E2
Antananarivo **51** D3
Antarctica **63**
Antigua and Barbuda **55** F1
Antofagasta **60** B2
Antrim **24** B1
Antrim Mountains **24** B1/B2
Appalachian Mountains **57** E2
Appennines *mountains* **42** D3
Arabian Peninsula **44** B4
Arabian Sea **46/47** B2
Arafura Sea **62** B3
Aral Sea **44** B5/C5
Ararat, Mount **38** E1
Arbroath **25** F3
Arctic Ocean **63**
Arequipa **60** B3
Argentina **59** B1/B2
Armagh **24** B1
Armenia **45** B5
Arnold **27** F2
Arran *island* **24** C2
Arun, River **29** D2
Arusha **53** B2
Ascension Island **51** A3
Ashford **29** E2
Ashgabat **45** B4
Asmara **51** C4
Astana **45** C5
Asuncion **61** D2
Atacama Desert **60** B2/B3
Athens **43** E2
Atlanta **57** E2
Atlantic Ocean **38** B2
Atlas Mountains **50** A5/B5
Auckland **62** D2
Australia **62** A2/C3
Austria **42** D3
Aviemore **23** F2
Avon, River **27** F2
Ayers Rock *mountain* **62** B2
Aylesbury **29** D2
Ayr **24** D2
Azerbaijan **45** B5
Azov, Sea of **43** F3

B

Baffin Bay **54** F4/G4
Baffin Island **54** E4/F4
Baghdad **45** B4
Bahamas, The **55** F2
Bahrain **45** B4
Baku **45** B5
Balearic Islands **42** C2
Bali *island* **44** E2
Balkhash, Lake **44** C5
Ballybofey **24** A1
Ballymena **24** B1
Ballymoney **24** B2
Baltic Sea **40/41** E2/F2
Bamako **51** A4
Banbridge **24** B1
Banbury **27** F2
Bandar Seri Begawan **45** E3
Bandung **45** E2
Bangalore **47** C2
Bangkok **45** E3
Bangladesh **47** D3/E3
Bangor *Northern Ireland* **24** C1
Bangor *Wales* **26** C3
Bangui **51** B4
Banjul **51** A4
Banks Island **54** C4/D4
Bann, River **24** B1
Barbados **55** G1
Barcelona **42** C3
Barents Sea **44** A6/B6
Barking **29** E2
Barmouth **26** C2
Barnet **29** D2
Barnstaple **30** C3
Barra *island* **22** B1/B2
Barrow-in-Furness **25** E1
Barrow, River **18**
Barry **26** D1
Basildon **29** E2
Basingstoke **31** F3
Bass Strait **62** C1/C2
Bath **31** E3
Baykal, Lake **44** E5
Beachy Head *cape* **29** E1
Beaufort Sea **54** B4/C4
Bedford **27** G2
Beijing **48** E3
Beira **51** C3
Beirut **45** A4
Belarus **41** F2/G2
Belem **61** E4
Belfast **24** C1
Belfast Lough *estuary* **24** C1
Belgium **40** D2
Belgrade **43** E3
Belize **55** E1
Belmopan **55** E1
Belo Horizonte **61** E2
Benbecula *island* **22** B2
Ben Cruachan *mountain* **24** C3
Bengal, Bay of **47** D2/E2
Benghazi **51** C5
Benin **51** B4
Ben Nevis *mountain* **22** D1
Benue, River **50** B4
Ben Wyvis *mountain* **22** E2
Bergen **40** D3
Bering Sea **44** J5
Bering Strait **44** J6
Berlin **40** E2
Bermuda *island* **55** F2
Bern **42** C3
Berneray *island* **22** B2
Berwick-upon-Tweed **25** F2
Bexley **29** E2
Bhutan **47** D3/E3
Bilbao **42** B3
Birkenhead **26** D3
Birmingham **27** F2
Biscay, Bay of **42** B3
Bishkek **45** C5
Bismarck Sea **62** C3
Bissau **51** A4
Blackburn **26** E3
Black Mountains **26** D1/D2
Blackpool **26** D3
Black Sea **43** E3/F3
Blackwater, River **18**
Blue Nile River **50** C4
Blyth **25** G2
Bodmin Moor **30** C2
Bognor Regis **29** D1
Bogota **60** B5
Bolivia **60/61** C3
Bolton **26** E3
Bordeaux **42** B3
Borneo *island* **44** E2/E3
Bornholm *island* **40** E2
Bosnia-Herzegovina **42/43** D3
Boston *UK* **27** G2
Boston *USA* **57** F3
Bothnia, Gulf of **38** C3/D3
Botswana **51** C2
Bournemouth **31** F2
Boyne, River **18**

C

Bradford **27** F3
Braemar **23** F2
Brahmaputra River **47** E3
Brasilia **61** E3
Bratislava **42** D3
Brazil **60/61**
Brazilian Highlands **61** E3
Brazzaville **51** B3
Brecon **26** D1
Brecon Beacons *mountains* **26** D1
Brent **29** D2
Bressay *island* **23** H5
Bridgend **26** D1
Bridgnorth **27** E2
Bridgwater **30** D3
Bridlington **25** H1
Brighton **29** D1
Brisbane **62** C2
Bristol **26** D1
Bristol Channel **30** C3/D3
Bromley **29** E2
Broome **62** B3
Brunei **45** E3
Brussels **40** D2
Bucharest **43** E3
Budapest **43** D3
Buenos Aires **59** C2
Bujumbura **51** C3
Bulgaria **43** E3
Bure, River **29** F3
Burkina **51** A4/B4
Burton upon Trent **27** F2
Burundi **51** C3
Bury **27** E3
Bury St. Edmunds **29** E3
Bute *island* **24** C2
Butt of Lewis *cape* **22** C3
Buxton **27** F3

C

Cabinda *admin.* **51** B3
Cadair Idris *mountain* **26** D2
Caernarfon **26** C3
Caerphilly **26** D1
Cairngorms *mountains* **23** F2
Cairns **62** C3
Cairo **52** C2
Calais **40** D2
Calgary **55** D3
Cali **60** B5
California, Gulf of **54** E2/F3
Cambodia **45** E3
Cambrian Mountains **26** D2
Cambridge **29** E3
Cameroon **51** B4
Cameroun, Mount **50** B4
Campbeltown **24** C2
Canada **55** C4/G3
Canadian Shield **54** E3/F3
Canary Islands **51** A5
Canberra **62** C2
Canna *island* **22** C2
Cannock **27** E2
Cantabrian Mountains **42** B3
Canterbury **29** F2
Cape Town **51** B2
Cape Verde **14** D3
Cape York Peninsula **62** C3
Caracas **59** B4
Cardiff **26** D1
Cardigan **26** C2
Cardigan Bay **26** C2
Caribbean Sea **54** F1
Carlisle **25** F1
Carmarthen **26** C1
Carn Eige *mountain* **22** D2
Carpathians *mountains* **43** E3
Carpentaria, Gulf of **62** B3/C3
Carrantuohill *mountain* **18**
Carrickfergus **24** C1
Casablanca **51** A5
Caspian Sea **44** B4/B5
Castleblayney **24** B1
Castle Douglas **25** E1
Castleford **27** F3
Caucasus *mountains* **38** E2
Cayenne **59** C4
Celebes Sea **44** E3/F3
Central African Republic **51** B4/C4
Central Russian Uplands **38** D2
Ceuta *territory* **42** B2
Chad **51** B4/C4
Chad, Lake **50** B4
Chang Jiang *river* **48** D2/D3
Channel Islands **31** E1
Chari, River **50** B4
Chelmsford **29** E2
Cheltenham **28** B2
Chelyabinsk **45** C5
Chennai **47** D2
Cherwell, River **28** C2
Chester **26** E3
Chesterfield **27** F3
Cheviot Hills **25** F2
Chicago **57** E3
Chile **59** B1/B2
Chiloé Island **58** B1

D

Chiltern Hills **28/29** C2/D2
Chimborazo *mountain* **60** B4
China **45** D4/F5
Chisinau **43** E3
Chongqing **48** D2
Chorley **26** E3
Christchurch **62** D1
Cirencester **28** C2
Citlaltepetl *mountain* **54** E1
Clydebank **24** D2
Clyde, River **25** E2
Coalville **27** F2
Coast Mountains **54** C3
Cocos Islands **58** A4
Cod, Cape **57** G3
Colombia **59** B3/B4
Colombo **47** C1
Colorado Plateau **56** B2
Colorado, River *Argentina* **58** B2
Colorado River *USA* **56** B2
Columbia River **56** A3/B3
Colwyn Bay *town* **26** D3
Comoros **51** D3
Conakry **51** A4
Concepcion **59** B2
Congo **51** B3/B4
Congo, Democratic Republic of **51** B3/C4
Congo, River **50** C4
Consett **25** G1
Conwy **26** D3
Cook, Mount **62** D1
Copenhagen **40** E2
Coquet, River **25** F2/G2
Coral Sea **62** C3
Corby **27** G2
Cordoba **61** C1
Cork **40** C2
Corsica *island* **42** C3
Costa Rica **55** E1
Côte d'Ivoire **51** A4
Cotopaxi *mountain* **60** B4
Cotswold Hills **28** B2/C2
Coventry **27** F2
Crawley **29** D2
Crete *island* **43** F2
Croatia **42/43** D3
Cromer **29** F3
Croydon **29** D2
Cuba **55** E2/F2
Cubango, River **50** B3
Cuillin Hills **22** C3
Cumbernauld **25** E2
Cumnock **24** D2
Cunene, River **50** B3
Cunnamula **62** C2
Curitiba **61** E2
Cwmbran **26** D1
Cyprus **43** G2
Czech Republic **40/41** E1/E2

D

Dakar **51** A4
Dalbeattie **25** E1
Dallas **57** D2
Damascus **45** B4
Danube, River **42/43** D3/E3
Dar es Salaam **51** C3
Darling, River **62** C2
Darlington **25** G1
Dartmoor **30** C2/D2
Dartmouth **30** D2
Dart, River **30** D2
Darwin **62** B3
Davis Strait **54** F4/G4
Dead Sea **44** A4
Deal **29** F2
Death Valley **56** B2
Deccan *plateau* **47** C2
Dee, River *Scotland* **23** G2
Dee, River *Wales* **26** D2/D3
Denbigh **26** D3
Denmark **40** D2/E2
Denmark Strait **54** H4
Denver **56** C2
Derby **27** F2
Derwent, River **27** F3
Detroit **57** E3
Deveron, River **23** G2
Devon Island **54** E4
Dhaka **47** E3
Dili **45** F2
Dinaric Alps *mountains* **42/43** D3
Dingwall **22** E2
Djibouti **51** D4
Djibouti **51** D4
Dniepr, River **41** G2
Dniester, River **41** F1
Dodoma **51** C3
Doha **45** B4
Dolgellau **26** D2

E

Dominica **55** F1
Dominican Republic **55** F1
Doncaster **27** F3
Donets'k **43** F3
Donets, River **38** C2
Don, River *England* **27** F3
Don, River *Russia* **41** H1
Don, River *Scotland* **23** G2
Dorchester **31** E2
Dornoch Firth *estuary* **23** E2/F2
Douglas **24** D1
Dover **29** F2
Downpatrick **24** C1
Drakensberg *mountains* **50** C2
Dublin **40** C2
Dudley **27** E2
Duero, River **42** B3
Dumbarton **24** D2
Dumfries **25** E2
Duncansby Head *cape* **23** F3
Dundalk **17**
Dundee **25** F3
Dunedin **62** D1
Dunfermline **25** E3
Dungannon **24** B1
Durban **51** C2
Durham **25** G1
Dushanbe **45** C4
Düsseldorf **40** D2
Dyfi, River **26** D2

E

Ealing **29** D2
Earn, River **25** E3
Eastbourne **29** E1
East China Sea **49** F2/F3
East Kilbride **24** D2
Eastleigh **31** F2
East Timor **45** F2
Ebro, River **42** B3
Ecuador **60** A4/B4
Eday *island* **23** G4
Eden, River **25** F1
Edinburgh **25** E2
Edmonton **55** D3
Egypt **52**
Eigg *island* **22** C1
Elbe, River **40** E2
Elbrus, Mount **38** E2
Elburz Mountains **44** B4
Elgin **23** F2
El Giza **52** C2
Ellesmere Island **54** E4/F5
El Salvador **55** E1
Ely **29** E3
Emi Koussi *mountain* **50** B5
Enfield **29** D2
England **20**
English Channel **17**
Enniskillen **24** A1
Equatorial Guinea **51** B4
Erie, Lake **57** E3/F3
Eritrea **51** C4/D4
Esfahan **45** B4
Esk, River **25** E2
Espiritu Santo *island* **62** D3
Estonia **41** F2
Ethiopia **51** C4/D4
Ethiopian Highlands **50** C4
Etna, Mount **42** D2
Euphrates, River **44** B4
Everest, Mount **48** B2
Evesham **27** F2
Exe, River **30** D3
Exeter **30** D2
Exmoor **30** D3
Exmouth **30** D2
Eyre, Lake **62** B2

F

Fair Isle *island* **23** H4
Falkirk **25** E2
Falkland Islands **59** B1/C1
Falmouth **30** B2
Fareham **31** F2
Farewell, Cape **54** G4
Faroe Islands **38** B3
Federated States of Micronesia **15** H3
Felixstowe **29** F2
Fetlar *island* **23** J5
Fiji **15** H2
Finisterre, Cape **42** B3
Finland **41** F3
Firth of Clyde *estuary* **24** C2/D2
Firth of Forth *estuary* **25** E3/F3
Firth of Lorn *estuary* **24** C3
Fishguard **26** C1
Fitzroy, River **62** B3
Fleetwood **26** D3
Flinders, River **62** C2/C3
Florence **42** D3
Folkestone **29** F2
Forel, Mount **54** H4
Forfar **23** F2
Fortaleza **61** F4
Fort Augustus **22** E2
Forth, River **24/25** D3/E3

Fort William **22** D1
Foula *island* **23** G5
Foyle, River **24** A1
France 42 B3/C3
Fraserburgh **23** G2
Fraser River **54** C3
Freetown **51** A4
French Guiana **59** C4
Frisian Islands **40** D2
Frome, River **31** E2
Fuji, Mount **49** G3
Fukuoka **49** G3

Gabon 51 B3/B4
Gaborone **51** C2
Galapagos Islands **59** A3
Galashiels **25** F2
Galway **40** C2
Gambia, The 51 A4
Ganges, River **47** C3/D3
Gateshead **25** G1
Geneva **42** C3
Georgetown **59** C4
Georgia 39 E2
Germany 40 D1/E2
Ghana 51 A4
Gibraltar *territory* **42** B2
Gibraltar, Strait of **38** B1
Gillingham **29** E2
Girvan **24** D2
Glasgow **24** D2
Glenrothes **25** E3
Gloucester **28** B2
Goat Fell *mountain* **24** C2
Gobi Desert **48** C4/D4
Gold Coast *town* **62** C2
Good Hope, Cape of **50** B2
Göteborg **40** E2
Gotland *island* **41** E2
Grampian Mountains **23** E1/F1
Grantham **27** G2
Gravesend **29** E2
Great Australian Bight *bay* **62** B2
Great Barrier Reef **62** C2/C3
Great Basin **56** B2
Great Bear Lake **54** C4/D4
Great Britain *islands* **18**
Great Dividing Range **62** C2/C3
Greater Antilles *islands* **54** E2/F1
Great Malvern **27** E2
Great Ouse, River **29** D3/E3
Great Plains **54** D3
Great Salt Lake **56** B3
Great Slave Lake **54** D4
Great Victoria Desert **62** B2
Great Yarmouth **29** F3
Greece 43 E2/E3
Greenland 55 F4/H4
Greenland Sea **38** B3
Greenock **24** D2
Grenada 55 F1
Greymouth **62** D1
Grimsby **27** G3
Guadalajara **55** D2
Guam 15 H3
Guangzhou **48** E2
Guatemala 55 E1
Guatemala **55** E1
Guayaquil **60** A4
Guernsey *island* **31** E1
Guiana Highlands **58** B4/C4
Guildford **29** D2
Guinea 51 A4
Guinea-Bissau 51 A4
Guinea, Gulf of **50** A4/B4
Guyana 59 C4

Haiti 55 F1
Halifax Canada **57** G3
Halifax UK **27** F3
Hamburg **40** E2
Hamersley Range *mountains* **62** A2
Hamilton New Zealand **62** D2
Hamilton UK **24** D2
Hanoi **48** D2
Harare **51** C3
Harbin **49** F4
Harlow **29** E2
Harris *island* **22** B2/C2
Harrogate **27** F3
Harrow **29** D2
Hartland Point *cape* **30** C3
Hartlepool **25** G1
Harwich **29** F2
Hastings **29** E1
Havana **55** E2
Havant **28** D1
Havering **29** E2
Hawick **25** F2
Hay-on-Wye **26** D2
Hekla, Mount **38** B3
Helsinki **41** F3
Hereford **26** E2
Herm *island* **31** E1
Herma Ness *cape* **23** J5
Hexham **25** F1
Hillingdon **29** D2
Himalaya *mountains* **47** C4/D3
Hindu Kush *mountains* **44** C4
Hispaniola *island* **54** F1
Hobart **62** C1
Hô Chi Minh **45** E3
Hoggar Mountains **50** B5
Hokkaido *island* **49** H4
Holyhead **26** C3
Holy Island **25** G2
Honduras 55 E1
Hong Kong **48** E2
Honiara **62** C3
Honshu *island* **49** G3/H4
Horn, Cape **58** B1
Horsham **29** D2
Hounslow **29** D2
Houston **57** D1
Hoy *island* **23** F3
Huang He *river* **48** D3/E3
Huddersfield **27** F3
Hudson Bay **54** E3/E4
Hudson River **54** F3
Hudson Strait **54** F4
Humber, River **27** G3
Hungary 42/43 D3/E3
Huron, Lake **57** E3
Hyderabad **47** C2

I

Ibiza *island* **42** C2
Iceland 40 A3/B3
Ilfracombe **30** C3
Ilkeston **27** F2
India 46/47
Indian Ocean **44** D2
Indonesia 45 E2/F2
Indus, River **46/47** B3/C4
Inner Hebrides *islands* **22** C1/C2
Inverness **23** E2
Iona *island* **24** B3
Ionian Sea **43** D2
Ipswich **29** F3
Iquitos **60** B4
Iran 45 B4
Iraq 45 B4
Ireland *island* **18**
Irrawaddy River **48** C1/C2
Irtysh, River **44** C5
Irvine **24** D2
Islamabad **47** C4
Islay *island* **24** B2
Isle of Man **24** D1
Isle of Wight **31** F2
Isles of Scilly **30** A1
Israel 45 A4
Istanbul **43** E3
Italy 42/43 C3/D3
Izmir **43** E2

J

Jakarta **45** E2
Jamaica 55 F1
Jammu and Kashmir *state* **47** C4
Japan 49 F2/H4
Japan, Sea of **49** G3/G4
Java *island* **44** E2
Java Sea **44** E2
Jaya Peak *mountain* **62** B3
Jedda **45** A4
Jersey *island* **31** E1
Jerusalem **45** A4
Johannesburg **51** C2
John o'Groats **23** F3
Jordan 45 A4
Juan Fernandez Islands **59** B2
Jura *island* **24** B2/C3
Jura *mountains* **38** C2
Jylland *peninsula* **38** C2

K

K2 *mountain* **47** C4
Kabul **46** B4
Kalahari Desert **50** B2/C2
Kalgoorlie **62** B2
Kaliningrad **41** F2
Kamchatka *peninsula* **44** G5/H5
Kampala **53** A3
Kansas City **57** D2
Karachi **46** B3
Kasai, River **50** B3
Kathmandu **47** D3
Kazakhstan 45 B5/D5
Kazakh Upland **44** C5
Kendal **25** F1
Kenya 53
Kenya, Mount **53** B2
Keswick **25** E1
Kettering **27** G2
Kharkov **41** G1
Khartoum **51** C4
Kidderminster **27** E2
Kielder Water *lake* **25** F2
Kiev **41** G2
Kigali **51** C3
Kilimanjaro, Mount **53** B2
Kilmarnock **24** D2
Kimberley Plateau **62** B3
Kinabalu **44** E3
King's Lynn **29** E3
Kingston Jamaica **55** F1
Kingston UK **29** D2
Kingston upon Hull **27** G3
Kinshasa **51** B3
Kiribati 14/15
Kirkcaldy **25** E3
Kirkcudbright **24** D1
Kirkwall **23** G3
Kisumu **53** A2
Kola Peninsula **38** D3/E3
Kolkata **47** D3
Kolyma, River **44** G6
Kosciusko, Mount **62** C2
Krákow **41** F2
Kuala Lumpur **45** E3
Kunlun Shan *mountains* **48** B3
Kuril Islands **45** G5
Kuwait 45 B4
Kuwait **45** B4
Kyle of Lochalsh **22** D2
Kyrgyzstan 45 C5
Kyushu *island* **49** G3

L

Laayoune **51** A5
Laccadive Islands **47** C1/C2
Ladoga, Lake **41** G3
Lagan, River **24** B1
Lagos **51** B4
Lahore **47** C4
Lake District *geog. reg.* **25** E1/F1
Lammermuir Hills **25** F2
Lancaster **25** F1
Land's End *cape* **30** B2
Lanzhou **48** D3
Laos 45 E3/E4
La Paz **60** C3
Lappland **38** D3
Larne **24** C1
Latvia 41 F2
Lebanon 45 A4
Leeds **27** F3
Leeuwin, Cape **62** A2
le Havre **40** D1
Leicester **27** F2
Lena, River **44** F6
Lerwick **23** H5
Lesotho 51 C2
Lesser Antilles *islands* **54** F1
Letterkenny **24** A1
Lewis *island* **22** C3
Liard River **54** C3/C4
Liberia 51 A4
Libreville **51** B4
Libya 51 B5/C5
Liechtenstein 42 C3
Liffey, River **18**
Lifford **24** A1
Lille **42** C4
Lilongwe **51** C3
Lima **60** B3
Limerick **17**
Limpopo, River **50** C2
Lincoln **27** G3
Lincoln Wolds *hills* **27** G3
Lisbon **42** B2
Lisburn **24** B1
Lithuania 41 F2
Little Minch *sound* **22** C2
Liverpool **26** E3
Livingston **25** E2
Ljubljana **42** D3
Llandovery **26** D1
Llandudno **26** D3
Llanelli **26** C1
Llangollen **26** D2
Loch Awe *lake* **24** C3
Loch Fyne *lake* **24** C2/C3
Loch Linnhe *lake* **24** C3
Loch Lomond *lake* **24** D3
Loch Ness *lake* **22** E2
Loch Rannoch *lake* **24** D3
Loch Shin *lake* **22** E3
Loch Tay *lake* **24** D3
Lofoten Islands **38** C3
Logan, Mount **54** B4
Loire, River **42** C3
Lomé **51** B4
London **29** D2
Londonderry **24** A1
Long Eaton **27** F2
Lord Howe Island **62** C2
Los Angeles **56** B2
Loughborough **27** F2
Lough Foyle *estuary* **24** A2
Lough Neagh *lake* **24** B1
Louth **27** G3
Lower Lough Erne *lake* **24** A1
Lowestoft **29** F3
Lualaba, River **50** C3
Luanda **51** B3
Lundy *island* **30** C3
Lune, River **25** F1
Lurgan **24** B1
Lusaka **51** C3
Luton **29** D2
Luxembourg 40 D1
Luxembourg **40** D1
Luzon *island* **44** F3
Lyme Bay **31** E2
Lyme Regis **30** E2
Lyons **42** C3
Lytham St. Anne's **26** D3

M

Mablethorpe **27** H3
Macclesfield **27** E3
Macdonnell Ranges *mountains* **62** B2
Macedonia, Former Yugoslav Republic of 43 E3
Mackenzie River **54** C4
Madagascar 51 D2/D3
Madeira *islands* **51** A5
Madeira, River **61** C4
Madrid **42** B3
Magdalena, River **58** B4
Maidstone **29** E2
Malabo **51** B4
Málaga **42** B2
Malawi 51 C3
Malay Peninsula **44** E3
Malaysia 45 E3
Maldives 45 C3
Malé **45** D3
Mali 51 A4/A5
Malin Head *cape* **24** A2
Mallaig **22** D2
Mallorca *island* **42** C2
Malmö **40** E2
Malta 42 D2
Malton **25** H1
Managua **55** E1
Manama **45** B4
Manaus **61** C4
Manchester **27** E3
Manila **45** F3
Maputo **51** C2
Maracaibo **59** B4
Maracaibo, Lake **58** B4
Mar del Plata **59** C2
Margate **29** F2
Marrakech **51** A5
Marseilles **42** C3
Marshall Islands 15
Maseru **51** C2
Mashhad **45** B4
Massif Central *mountains* **42** C3
Mato Grosso *geog. reg.* **61** D3
Mauritania 51 A4/A5
Mauritius 15 F2
Mbabane **51** C2
Mbeya **53** A1
McKinley, Mount **54** B4
Medan **45** D3
Medellin **59** B4
Mediterranean Sea **42/43** C2/F2
Medway, River **29** E2
Mekong River **48** D2
Melbourne **62** C2
Melilla *territory* **42** B2
Mendip Hills **31** E3
Menorca *island* **42** C2/C3
Mersey, River **26** E3
Merthyr Tydfil **26** D1
Merton **29** D2
Mexico 55 D2/E1
Mexico City **55** E1
Mexico, Gulf of **54** E2
Miami **57** E1
Michigan, Lake **57** E3
Middlesbrough **25** G1
Milan **42** C3
Milford Haven **26** B1
Milton Keynes **27** G2
Mindanao *island* **44** F3
Mindoro *island* **44** F3
Minehead **30** D3
Mingulay *island* **22** B1
Minneapolis **57** D3
Minsk **41** F2
Mississippi River **57** D2
Missouri River **56/57** B3/D2
Moffat **25** E2
Mogadishu **51** D4
Moldova 43 E3
Mombasa **53** B2
Monaco 42 C3
Monadhliath Mountains **23** E2/F2
Monaghan **24** B1
Mongolia 48 C4/E4
Monmouth **26** E1
Monrovia **51** A4
Mont Blanc *mountain* **42** C3
Montenegro 43 D3
Monterray **57** C1
Montréal **57** F3
Montrose **25** F3
Moray Firth *estuary* **23** E2/F2
Morecambe **25** F1
Morocco 51 A5
Morogoro **53** B1
Moroni **51** D3
Moscow **41** G2
Montevideo **59** C2
Motherwell **25** D2
Mount Isa *town* **62** B2
Mourne Mountains **24** B1
Mozambique 51 C2/C3
Mozambique Channel **50** C2/D3
Mull *island* **24** B3/C3
Mull of Galloway *cape* **24** D1
Mull of Kintyre *cape* **24** C2
Mumbai **47** C2
Munich **40** E1
Murmansk **41** G3
Murray, River **62** C2
Muscat **46** A3
Mwanza **53** A2
Myanmar 48 C1/C2

N

Nairobi **53** B2
Namib Desert **50** B2
Namibia 51 B2/B3
Naples **42** D3
Nassau **55** F2
Nasser, Lake **52** C1
Nauru 15 H2
Ndjamena **51** B4
Neath **26** D1
Negro, River Argentina **58** B2
Negro, River Brazil **60/61** C4
Nene, River **29** D3/E3
Nepal 47 D3
Netherlands 40 D2
Newark-on-Trent **27** G3
Newbury **31** F3
Newcastle **62** C2
Newcastle upon Tyne **25** G1
New Delhi **47** C3
Newfoundland *island* **54** G3
New Guinea *island* **62** B3/C3
New Orleans **57** D1
Newport **26** E1
New Quay **26** C2
Newquay **30** B2
Newry **24** B1
Newtown **26** D2
Newtownabbey **24** C1
Newtownards **24** C1
New York **57** F3
New Zealand 62 D1/D2
Niamey **51** B4
Nicaragua 55 E1
Nicaragua, Lake **54** E1
Nice **42** C3
Nicobar Islands **45** D3
Nicosia **43** F2
Nidd, River **25** G1
Niger 51 B4
Nigeria 51 B4
Niger, River **50** A4/B4
Nile, River **52** C1/C3
Nith, River **25** E2
Nizhniy-Novgorod **41** H2
Northallerton **25** G1
Northampton **27** G2
North Channel **24** C1/C2
North Downs *hills* **29** D2/E2
North Dvina, River **38** E3
Northern Ireland **24** A1/C1
Northern Marianas 15 H3
North Esk, River **23** G1
North European Plain **41** E2/F2
North Island **62** D2
North Korea 49 F3/F4
North Ronaldsay *island* **23** G4
North Sea **40** D2
North Uist *island* **22** B2
Northwest Highlands **22** D2/E3
North York Moors **25** H1
Norway 40/41 D2/F4
Norwich **29** F3
Nottingham **27** F2
Nouakchott **51** A4
Noumea **62** D2
Novosibirsk **45** D5
Nullarbor Plain **62** B2
Nuuk **55** G4
Nyasa, Lake **50** C3

O

Oban **24** C3
Ob', River **44** C6
Oder, River **40** E2
Odessa **43** F3
Ohio River **57** E2
Ojos del Salado *mountain* **60** C2
Okhotsk, Sea of **44** G5
Okovango Swamp **50** C3
Oldham **27** E3
Olympus, Mount **43** E3
Omagh **24** A1
Oman 45 B3/B4
Omsk **45** C5
Onega, Lake **41** G3
Ontario, Lake **57** F3
Oporto **42** B3
Orange, River **50** B2/C2
Orinoco, River **58** B4

80 Index

Orkney Islands 23 F3/G4
Osaka 49 G3
Oslo 40 E2
Oswestry 26 D2
Ottawa 57 F3
Ouagadougou 51 A4
Oubangui, River 50 B4
Ouse, River 27 F3
Outer Hebrides *islands* 22 B1/C3
Oxford 28 C2

P
Pabbay *island* 22 B2
Pacific Ocean 64/65
Paisley 24 D2
Pakistan 46/47 B3/C4
Palau 15 H3
Palembang 45 E2
Panama 55 E1/F1
Panama City 55 F1
Papa Westray *island* 23 G4
Papua New Guinea 62 C3
Paraguay 61 C2/D2
Paraguay, River 61 D2
Paramaribo 59 C4
Paraná, River 58 B2/C2
Paris 42 C3
Parry Islands 54 D4
Peace River 54 D3
Pechora, River 38 E3
Peipus, Lake 41 F2
Peloponnese *islands* 43 E2
Pemba Island 53 B1
Pennines *hills* 25 F1
Penrith 25 F1
Pentland Firth *sound* 23 F3
Penzance 30 B2
Perm 45 B5
Perth Australia 62 A2
Perth UK 25 E3
Peru 60 B3/B4
Peterborough 27 G2
Peterhead 23 H2
Philadelphia 57 F2
Philippines 45 F3
Phnom Penh 45 E3
Phoenix 56 B2
Pilcomayo, River 61 C2/D2
Pindus Mountains 43 E2/E3
Pittsburgh 57 F3
Plymouth 30 C2
Poland 40/41 E2/F2
Pontypool 26 D1
Poole 31 F2
Poopo, Lake 60 C3
Popocatepetl *mountain* 54 E1
Po, River 42 D3
Portadown 24 B1
Port Augusta 62 B2
Port-au-Prince 55 F1
Portland 56 A3
Portland Bill *cape* 31 E2
Port Moresby 62 C3
Porto Alegre 61 D1
Porto Novo 51 B4
Portree 22 C2
Portsmouth 31 F2
Port Talbot 26 D1
Portugal 42 B2/B3
Port Vila 62 D3
Prague 40 E2
Preston 26 E3
Pretoria 51 C2
Príncipe *island* 50 B4
Puebla 55 E1
Puerto Rico 55 F1
Punta Arenas 59 B1
Pusan 49 F3
Pwllheli 26 C2
Pyongyang 49 F3
Pyrénées *mountains* 42 C3

Q
Qatar 45 B4
Quantock Hills 30 D3
Québec 57 F3
Queen Charlotte Islands 54 C3
Quezon City 45 F3
Quito 60 B4
Qullai Garmo *mountain* 44 C4

R
Raasay *island* 22 C2
Rabat 51 A5
Ras Dashen Terara *mountain* 50 C4
Rathlin Island 24 B2
Reading 28 D2
Recife 61 F4
Redbridge 29 E2
Redcar 25 G1
Redditch 27 F2
Redhill 29 D2
Red Sea 50 C5/D4
Reigate 29 D2
Republic of Ireland 40 C2
Republic of South Africa 51 B2/C2
Reykjavik 40 A3
Rhine, River 40 D1

Rhodes *island* 43 E2
Rhondda 26 D1
Rhône, River 42 C3
Rhum *island* 22 C1/C2
Ribble, River 27 E3
Richmond 25 G1
Rift Valley 50 C3/C4
Riga 41 F2
Rio de Janeiro 61 E2
Rio de la Plata *river* 58 C2
Rio Grande 56/57 C2/D1
Ripon 25 G1
Riyadh 45 B4
Rocas Island 59 D3
Rochdale 27 E3
Rockhampton 62 C2
Rocky Mountains 54 C3/D2
Romania 43 E3
Rome 42 D3
Roraima, Mount 58 B4
Rosario 59 B2
Rosslare 17
Rostov-on-Don 43 F3
Rotherham 27 F3
Rotterdam 40 D2
Rousay *island* 23 F4/G4
Royal Tunbridge Wells 29 E2
Rugby 27 F2
Runcorn 26 E3
Russian Federation 45 A5/J6
Ruwenzori, Mount 50 C3/C4
Rwanda 51 C3
Rybinsk Reservoir 41 G2
Ryukyu Islands 49 F2

S
Sacramento 56 A2
Sahara Desert 50 A5/C5
St. Abb's Head *cape* 25 F2
St. Albans 29 D2
St. Andrews 25 F3
St. Austell 30 C2
St. Bees Head *cape* 25 E1
St. David's Head *cape* 26 B1
St. George's Channel 26 A1/B2
St. Helena *island* 51 A3
St. Helens 26 E3
St. Ives 30 B2
St. Kilda *island* 22 A2
St. Kitts and Nevis 55 F1
St. Lawrence, Gulf of 54 F3/G3
St. Lawrence River 54 F3
St. Louis 57 D2
St. Lucia 55 F1
St. Peter Port 31 E1
St. Petersburg 41 G2
St-Pierre & Miquelon *islands* 55 G3
St. Vincent and the Grenadines 55 F1
St. Vincent, Cape 42 B2
Sakhalin *island* 44 G5
Salisbury 31 F3
Salisbury Plain *hills* 31 F3
Salt Lake City 56 B3
Salvador 61 F3
Salween River 48 C2
Samoa 14 A2
Sana 45 B3
Sanday *island* 23 G4
San Diego 56 B2
San Francisco 56 A2
San José 55 E1
San Juan 55 F1
San Marino 42 D3
San Salvador 55 E1
Santa Cruz 61 C3
Santa Cruz Islands 62 D3
Santander 42 B3
Santiago 59 B2
Santo Domingo 55 F1
São Francisco, River 61 E3
São Paulo 61 E2
São Tomé 51 B4
São Tomé and Principe 51 B4
Sapporo 49 H4
Sarajevo 43 D3
Sardinia *island* 42 C2/C3
Sark *island* 31 E1
Saskatchewan River 54 D3
Saudi Arabia 45 B3/B4
Sawel *mountain* 24 A1
Scafell Pike *mountain* 25 E1
Scalloway 23 H5
Scalpay *island* 22 C2
Scandinavia 38 C3
Scarborough 25 H1
Scotland 20/20
Scunthorpe 27 G3
Seattle 56 A3
Seine, River 42 C3
Semarang 45 E2
Senegal 51 A4
Senegal River 50 A4
Seoul 49 F3
Serbia 733 E3/F3
Severn, River 28 B2/B3
Seville 42 B2
Seychelles 15

Sgurr Mór *mountain* 22 D2
Shanghai 49 F3
Shannon, River 18
Shapinsay *island* 23 G4
Sheerness 29 E2
Sheffield 27 F3
Shenyang 49 F4
Shetland Islands 23 H4/J5
Shiraz 45 B4
Shrewsbury 26 D2
Siberian Lowland 44 C5/D6
Sicily *island* 42 D2
Sidlaw Hills 25 E3/F3
Sierra Leone 51 A4
Sierra Madre Occidental *mountains* 54 D2
Sierra Madre Oriental *mountains* 54 D2
Sierra Nevada *mountains* 56 A2/B2
Sinai, Mount 52 C2
Singapore 45 E3
Skegness 27 H3
Skipton 27 E3
Skopje 43 E3
Skye *island* 22 C2/D2
Sleat, Sound of 22 D2
Slieve Donard *mountain* 24 C1
Slough 29 D2
Slovakia 40/41 E1/F1
Slovenia 42 D3
Snaefell *mountain* 24 D1
Snake River 56 B3
Snowdon *mountain* 26 C3
Soar, River 27 F2
Socotra 45 B3
Sofia 43 E3
Solihull 27 F2
Solomon Islands 62 C3/D3
Solway Firth *estuary* 25 E1
Somalia 51 D4
Sound of Jura 24 C2/C3
Southampton 31 F2
South China Sea 48/49 E1
South Downs *hills* 29 D1
Southend-on-Sea 29 E2
Southern Alps *mountains* 62 D1
Southern Ocean 63
Southern Uplands *mountains* 24/25 D2/E2
South Esk, River 25 F3
South Georgia *island* 59 D1
South Korea 49 F3
Southport 26 D3
South Ronaldsay *island* 23 G3
South Island 62 D1
South Uist *island* 22 B2
Southwold 29 F3
Spain 42 B2/B3
Spalding 27 G2
Sperrin Mountains 24 A1
Spey, River 23 F2
Spurn Head *cape* 27 H3
Sri Lanka 45 D3
Stafford 27 E2
Stanley 59 C1
Start Point *cape* 30 D2
Stavanger 40 D2
Stirling 25 E3
Stockholm 40 E2
Stockport 27 E3
Stockton-on-Tees 25 G1
Stoke-on-Trent 27 E3
Stornoway 22 C3
Strabane 24 A1
Strait of Dover 29 F1/F2
Strangford Lough *estuary* 24 C1
Stranraer 24 C1
Strasbourg 42 C3
Stratford-upon-Avon 27 F2
Stromness 23 F3
Stronsay *island* 23 G4
Stroud 31 E3
Sucre 61 C3
Sudan 51 C4
Suir, River 18
Sulawesi *island* 44 E2/F2
Sumatra *island* 44 E2/F2
Sumburgh Head *cape* 23 H4
Sunderland 25 G1
Superior, Lake 57 D3/E3
Surabaya 45 E2
Suriname 59 C4
Sutton 29 D2
Sutton Coldfield 27 F2
Swale, River 25 G1
Swanage 31 F2
Swansea 26 D1
Swaziland 51 C2
Sweden 40/41 E2/F3
Swindon 31 F3
Switzerland 42 C3
Sydney 62 C2
Syria 45 A4

T
Tabriz 45 B4
Tagus, River 42 B2

Taipei 49 F2
Taiwan 49 F2
Tajikistan 45 C4
Tallinn 41 F2
Tamar, River 30 C2
Tampere 41 F3
Tanganyika, Lake 50 C3
Tanzania 51 C3
Tapajos, River 61 D4
Tarbat Ness *cape* 23 F2
Tashkent 45 C5
Tasmania *island* 62 C1
Tasman Sea 62 D2
Taunton 30 D3
Taurus Mountains 43 F2
Taw, River 30 C2
Tay, River 25 E3
T'bilisi 39 E2
Tees, River 25 F1/G1
Tegucigalpa 55 E1
Tehran 45 B4
Teifi, River 26 C2
Teign, River 30 D2
Telford 26 D2
Teme, River 28 B3
Tennant Creek *town* 62 B3
Tennessee River 57 E2
Test, River 31 F3
Thailand 45 D3/E3
Thailand, Gulf of 44 E3
Thames, River 31 F3/G3
Thar Desert 47 C3
The Cheviot *mountain* 25 F2
The Fens *geog. reg.* 29 D3/E3
The Great Lakes 57 D3/F3
The Gulf 44 B4
The Hague 40 D2
The Minch *sound* 22 C3/D3
Thetford 29 E3
The Wash *estuary* 29 E3
Thimphu 47 D3
Thurso 23 F3
Thurso, River 23 F3
Tianjin 48 E3
Tibesti Mountains 50 B5
Tibet, Plateau of 48 B3/C3
Tien Shan *mountains* 48 A4/B4
Tierra del Fuego *island* 58 B1
Tigris, River 44 B4
Timor *island* 44 F2
Timor Sea 62 B3
Tiranë 43 D3
Tiree *island* 24 B3
Titicaca, Lake 60 C3
Tiverton 30 D2
Tocantins, River 61 E3/E4
Togo 51 B4
Tokyo 49 G3
Tom Price, Mount 62 A2
Tonga 14 A2
Torbay 30 D2
Toronto 57 F3
Torrens, Lake 62 B2
Townsville 62 C3
Trent, River 27 F2/G3
Trevose Head *cape* 30 B2
Trinidad and Tobago 55 F1
Tripoli 51 B5
Trowbridge 31 E3
Trujillo 60 B4
Truro 30 B2
Tunis 51 B5
Tunisia 51 B5
Turkana, Lake 53 B3
Turkey 39 D1/E2
Turkmenistan 45 B4/C4
Tuvalu 15 H2
Tweed, River 25 E2/F2
Tynemouth 25 G2
Tyne, River 25 G1
Tyrrhenian Sea 42 D2/D3
Tywi, River 26 D1

U
Ucayali, River 60 B4
Uganda 51 C4
Ujung Pandang 45 E2
Ukraine 43 E3/F4
Ulan Bator 48 D4
Ullapool 22 D2
Ullswater *lake* 25 F1
Ulva *island* 24 B3
United Arab Emirates 45 B4
United Kingdom 40 C2/C3
United States of America 56/57
Unst *island* 23 J5
Upper Lough Erne *lake* 24 A1
Ural Mountains 38 E2/E3
Ure, River 25 G1
Uruguay 59 C2
Uruguay, River 58 C2
Urumqi 48 B4
Usk, River 26 D1
Uzbekistan 45 B5/C5

V
Vaal, River 50 C2
Valdés Peninsula 58 B1

Valencia Spain 42 B2
Valencia Venzuela 59 B4
Valletta 42 D2
Vancouver 56 A3
Vancouver Island 54 C3
Vänern, Lake 40 E2
Van, Lake 38 E1
Vanuatu 62 D3
Varanasi 47 D3
Vättern, Lake 40 E2
Venezuela 59 B4
Victoria Island 54 D4
Victoria, Lake 50 C3
Vienna 40 E2
Vientiane 48 D1
Vietnam 45 E3/E4
Venice 42 D3
Vilnius 41 F2
Vistula, River 41 E2
Volga, River 41 H2
Volta, Lake 50 A4/B4
Vyrnwy, River 26 D2

W
Wales 26
Walsall 27 F2
Waltham Forest *town* 29 E2
Walvis Bay *town* 51 B2
Warrenpoint 24 B1
Warrington 26 E3
Warsaw 41 F2
Warwick 27 F2
Washington 25 G1
Washington D.C. 57 F2
Waterford 17
Watford 29 D2
Waveney, River 29 F3
Wear, River 25 F1
Welland, River 27 G2
Wellington 62 D1
Wells-next-the-Sea 29 E3
Welwyn Garden City 29 D2
Wensum, River 29 F3
West Bromwich 27 F2
Western Sahara 51 A5
West Indies *islands* 54 F1/F2
Weston-super-Mare 30 E3
Westray *island* 23 F4/G4
Weymouth 31 E2
Whalsay *island* 23 H5/J5
Whernside *mountain* 25 F1
Whitby 25 H1
Whitehaven 25 E1
White Nile River 50 C4
White Sea 38 D3
Whitney, Mount 56 B2
Wick *lake* 23 F3
Wicklow Mountains 18
Widnes 26 E3
Wigan 26 E3
Wigtown 24 D1
Wilhem, Mount 62 C3
Winchester 31 F3
Windermere *lake* 25 F1
Windhoek 51 B2
Windsor 29 D2
Winnipeg 57 D3
Winnipeg, Lake 54 E3
Wisbech 29 E3
Witham, River 27 G3
Woking 29 D2
Wollongong 62 C2
Wolverhampton 27 E2
Worcester 27 E2
Workington 25 E1
Worksop 27 F3
Worthing 29 D1
Wrath, Cape 22 D3
Wrexham 26 E3
Wuhan 48 E3
Wye, River 26 D2

X
Xi'an 48 D3
Xiamen 49 E2

Y
Yamoussoukro 51 A4
Yangon 48 C1
Yaounde 51 B4
Yell *island* 23 H5
Yellow Sea 49 F3
Yemen Republic 45 B3
Yenisey River 44 D6
Yeo, River 31 E2
Yeovil 31 E2
Yerevan 45 C5
Yes Tor *mountain* 30 C2
York 27 F3
Yorkshire Wolds *hills* 25 H1
Yucatan Peninsula 54 E1/E2
Yukon River 54 B4

Z
Zagreb 42 D3
Zagros Mountains 44 B4
Zambezi, River 50 C3
Zambia 51 C3
Zanzibar *island* 50 B1
Zimbabwe 53 C2/C3

© Oxford University Press

World Flags

 Afghanistan

 Albania

 Algeria

 Andorra

 Angola

 Antigua and Barbuda

 Argentina

 Armenia

 Australia

 Austria

 Azerbaijan

 Bahamas

 Bahrain

 Bangladesh

 Barbados

 Belarus

 Belgium

 Belize

 Benin

 Bhutan

 Bolivia

 Bosnia-Herzegovina

 Botswana

 Brazil

 Brunei

 Bulgaria

 Burkina

 Burundi

 Cambodia

 Cameroon

 Canada

 Cape Verde

 Central African Republic

 Chad

 Chile

 China

 Colombia

 Comoros

 Congo

 Congo, Dem. Rep.

 Costa Rica

 Côte d'Ivoire

 Croatia

 Cuba

 Cyprus

 Czech Republic

 Denmark

 Djibouti

 Dominica

 Dominican Republic

 East Timor

 Ecuador

 Egypt

 El Salvador

 Equatorial Guinea

 Eritrea

 Estonia

 Ethiopia

 Fiji

 Finland

 France

 French Guiana

 Gabon

 Gambia

 Georgia

 Germany

 Ghana

 Greece

 Greenland

 Grenada

 Guatemala

 Guinea

 Guinea-Bissau

 Guyana

 Haiti

 Honduras

 Hungary

 Iceland

 India

 Indonesia

 Iran

 Iraq

 Ireland

 Israel

 Italy

 Jamaica

 Japan

 Jordan

 Kazakhstan

 Kenya

 Kiribati

 Kosovo

 Kuwait

 Kyrgyzstan

 Laos

 Latvia

 Lebanon

 Lesotho

© Oxford University Press